EVE *of* DESTRUCTION

Is There Hope for America?

by DAVID CERULLO

EVE *of* DESTRUCTION
Is There Hope for America?
by David Cerullo

Copyright © 2008 David Cerullo

Inspiration Ministries
P.O. Box 7750
Charlotte, NC 28241 USA

ISBN Number: 978-1-887600-90-3

Printed in the United States of America.

All Scripture passages are from the New American Standard Bible, unless otherwise noted.

New American Standard Bible © The Lockman Foundation, 1960.

2 3 4 5 6 7 8

TABLE OF CONTENTS

DEDICATION

This book is dedicated with great affection and appreciation to two of my friends and colleagues who understand my heart and without whose input, guidance, and help, this book would still be a message waiting to be written. Thank you, John Roos and Karen White, for the countless hours you've invested with me on this book. May our collaborative efforts accomplish the purpose for which God birthed this message in my heart.

"How did the Church
lose her influence and
spiritual power in this
part of the world?"

Introduction

A WAKEUP CALL!

IT BEGAN AS A PLEASANT CONVERSATION WITH OUR Muslim tour guide in Istanbul, Turkey. But after a few questions, the man made a statement that not only startled me; it shook me to my very core. In fact, I doubt I will ever be able to erase his ominous words from my mind.

Let me give you a little background...

My wife, Barbara, and I journeyed to Turkey and Greece on a tour tracing the steps of the Apostle Paul. The experience was wonderful, and as we traveled, we wondered what it must have been like for him on his missionary journeys.

We visited Ephesus, where Paul spent a year and a half in ministry. We sat in the outdoor theater where they had dragged some of the disciples when the whole city was in an uproar (Acts 19). We saw what was left of the harbor, and we walked up the road leading into the city, imagining Aquila and Priscilla hurrying along that same street to meet Paul. We even hiked up to the cave where the apostle had reportedly lived while in Ephesus.

From this new perspective, it was riveting to read the words of Jesus in Revelation to the church at Ephesus:

Unto the angel of the church of Ephesus write; These things saith he that holdeth the seven stars in his right hand, who walketh in the midst of the seven golden candlesticks; I know thy works, and thy labour, and thy patience, and how thou canst not bear them which are evil: and thou hast tried them which say they are apostles, and are not, and hast found them liars: And hast borne, and hast patience, and for my name's sake hast laboured, and hast not fainted.

Nevertheless I have somewhat against thee, because thou hast left thy first love. Remember therefore from whence thou art fallen, and repent, and do the first works; or else I will come unto thee quickly, and will remove thy candlestick out of his place, except thou repent" (Revelation 2:1-5 KJV).

Tragically, what Jesus had warned in this passage is exactly what happened. Ephesus – once a thriving city and one of the largest in the known world – now lies in ruins. There is no semblance of a church remaining. Their candlestick was, in fact, removed.

We visited Pergamum in Greece and saw the pagan altar John referred to as *"Satan's throne"* (Revelation 2:12-13). Athens was incredible as we stood atop Mars Hill and looked down on the Areopagus where Paul preached his message about the unknown God (Acts 17).

At Corinth and many other locations, we produced programs for our daily television flagship program, which has been meaningful to our Partners and viewers around the world.

I FELT LED TO STOP

Istanbul, Turkey, proved to be an amazing experience, for more than one reason. Here, in the ancient city of

Constantinople, the Church once flourished and was at one time considered the center of Christianity. Now Turkey is a Muslim country with a Christian population of less than 2%.

It was here that Constantine had built the *Hagia Sophia,* once the largest church on the face of the earth and the first domed structure to be engineered. But sadly, what was then a "church" eventually became a Muslim mosque. Now it's simply a museum to be toured instead of a cathedral in which to worship the Lord.

As Barbara and I gazed in amazement at this architectural wonder, we asked one another in dismay, "How did the Church lose her influence and spiritual power in this part of the world?"

One evening as we were headed back to our hotel, we were walking down the middle of the street flanked by the Blue Mosque on one side (one of the largest Muslim mosques in the world) and the *Hagia Sophia* on the other. I felt led to stop. We had been so burdened while on this trip for the precious people of Turkey and Greece – their spiritual emptiness and their need for Christ – that we often would pray together, "Lord, how can you use *us* to help reach these people with the Gospel?"

Our Inspiration Network International (INI) had recently launched its signal, and everywhere we traveled on this trip, we saw rooftops dotted with satellite dishes. We knew this "power of the air" was one of the greatest tools to reach Turkey and the Muslim people. In every city, we would pray for the Gospel to penetrate the hearts of the people for revival and salvation.

So there in the middle of the street in Istanbul, I felt impressed by the Lord to stop and pray once more. With the hustle and bustle of people all around us, I put my arm around Barbara's shoulder and said, "Let's pray."

We began to intercede for the people of Turkey, crying out for God to open their eyes spiritually so they would know the love of Christ and to make Him their Lord. We began praying in the Spirit together, and when we did, it suddenly seemed as if a spiritual earthquake were taking place. I've never felt anything like it before or since. It was similar to when you drop a stone into a pond, and you see the ripple effect moving outward from where you dropped the stone, circle after circle.

That's what I felt was happening spiritually. Something awesome was taking place in the spirit realm. It was as if heavenly forces were being realigned. I don't understand the full significance of what we were experiencing, but Barbara and I both felt it. Somehow, someway, God was at work when we released His power through our prayers on that street in Istanbul.

A DISTURBING ANSWER

One day later we were standing almost on the same spot with our tour guide. He was a young man in his late 20s or early 30s. Good looking, intelligent, articulate, polite, respectful, clean cut, friendly. On the surface he looked "normal."

Our group stopped between the *Hagia Sophia* and the Blue Mosque to ask him a few questions.

"Are you Muslim?" I began.

"Yes, I am," he replied.

"Do you read the Koran?

"Of course. Every day!"

"Do you pray to Allah?" I wanted to know.

"Absolutely – five times every day," he proudly responded.

I continued, "Do you believe what the Koran teaches?"

"Yes," he answered.

"Then to you we must be infidels," I commented.

He paused, thinking to himself for a moment, then answered, "Oh, no. You are clients."

I pressed the matter further. "Well doesn't the Koran teach that all non-Believers, especially Christians and Jews, are infidels?"

"Well, yes," he quietly replied.

"And doesn't the Koran teach that all non-Believers are to convert to Islam? Either submit...or die?"

Slowly, he responded, "Yes."

"Then if you heard an imam (a Muslim holy man) sounding out a call to Holy War – a Jihad – from one of these minarets, would you do everything within your power to kill us?"

I am sure he had never been asked such a direct question before. He looked at us, paused for a moment, and then without another hesitation said, "Yes, I would."

We stopped asking questions and moved on to our next stop in the tour for the day. As we did, we looked at one another in shock, stunned by the truth that someone who seemed to be as respectful and friendly as the "boy next door" could tell us to our faces that if called upon, he would do everything in his power to kill us!

As you will learn in this book, this is the tip of the iceberg of what the West is up against – here in America and in other western nations.

Are we on the Eve of Destruction? If so, how did we arrive at this alarming place? What can we do to change our world? *Is there hope for America?*

I have been shocked by
how America has drifted
so far from the moral
precepts we used to take
for granted. And I have
been deeply concerned
about our country.

Chapter One

A SPIRIT OF APATHY

FORTY-ONE PERCENT OF "BORN AGAIN" CHRISTIANS in America did not vote in the 2000 presidential elections!

Think about this fact for a moment. Let it sink into your heart and mind. Yes, 41% – more than two out of every five people who claim to be born again – chose not to vote!

Who were these people? In the survey, they said they were members of our churches who believed in God and read the Bible. They said they were followers of Jesus, prayed, and shared their faith with others. Some, no doubt, were pastors, Sunday school teachers, and church leaders. Millions of these Christians were concerned with the direction in which our nation was heading:

* They wanted prayer back in schools and students to be taught that God created the world.

* They opposed court rulings that eliminated the Ten Commandments from public buildings.

* They wanted Americans to be free to share their faith without being persecuted.

* They supported the sanctity of life and wanted to eliminate abortions.

* They were concerned about the declining moral standards in the media.

* They wanted leadership in our country that stood for Biblical principles.

* They were tired of laws being passed which endorsed homosexuality.

* They believed America was drifting further away from its Christian foundations.

* They believed Israel is the nation of God's Chosen People and that America should stand in support of Israel.

Yet, when it came time to vote, they sat back and did nothing!

The more I pondered this fact, the more troubled I became. I, too, have been outraged by efforts to eliminate the influence of the Christian faith from our public life. I have been shocked by how America has drifted so far from the moral precepts we used to take for granted. And I have been deeply concerned about our country.

But why would any Christian not vote? This seems the least we can do. Voting is our privilege as Americans and our responsibility as Believers. What kind of message does our lack of involvement send to the world? And to God?

I was overwhelmed with an obligation to do whatever I could to make a difference and help wake up Christian America. This is why in the days leading up to the 2004 elections, Barbara, and I hosted a month-long series of *Inspiration Today!* programs focusing on the importance of our national elections and the need for our nation to return to righteousness.

We talked with politicians of both parties. We interviewed educators, pastors, scholars, and business leaders. And although these influential guests may have had differences of opinion, they all agreed that Christians held the destiny and future of our nation in their hands.

Others joined us in a nation-wide campaign to encourage Christians to vote, and our efforts paid off. More people voted in the 2004 elections than in 2000. Pollsters, commentators, and politicians of both parties all subsequently agreed that Christians made a difference in the...

* people who were elected

* policies that were set by our government

* laws that were passed

* judges who were appointed and the rulings that they made

Yet even in 2004, with so much at stake, millions of Christians still chose not to vote!

Since that time, my concerns about our nation's future have continued to grow. Yes, Christians have experienced small victories but the slide toward immorality and judgment has not stopped. In fact, it is becoming an avalanche!

WHO IS AT FAULT?

Millions of Christians continue to sit on the sidelines. Maybe they don't know what to do. Perhaps they're busy or don't think their vote really matters. Or maybe they don't realize things are that bad.

But things are *that* bad. In fact, we face a crisis. On this point, the Bible is crystal clear: The judgment of God on our country is inevitable...*unless* we return to Him, repent, make serious changes, and return to righteousness (Leviticus 18:24-30).

Who is at fault? We can't blame the court system or politicians. Based on the Word of God, we have no one to blame but ourselves. If we want to bring America back to God and greatness, Christians cannot remain silent. *We* must change. *We* must vote. *We* must repent. *We* must pray and intercede for America. And *we* also must speak out and let our voice be heard! This is what I am doing in this book.

AMAZED AND SHOCKED!

God has given me the opportunity to have access to a wide range of information, to travel throughout the world, and to work with (and interview) many leaders within the business and Christian environments.

From my position as Chairman and CEO of Inspiration Ministries, I have developed wonderful relationships with people throughout the Church and many ministries. I've read countless research documents, from both secular and Christian sources, and have been given access to confidential materials from governments and ministries.

> If we want to bring America back to God and greatness, Christians cannot remain silent.

But none of this has prepared me for what I've seen with my own eyes, things I never imagined would happen in our country. I've followed with amazement what Christians are willing to believe:

* ⭐ I've seen Biblical standards ignored and even violently repressed (to the point that people

actually have been arrested in this country for praying or sharing their testimony).

* I've watched as our courts pushed Christianity out of our schools and our public life.

* I've been shocked that our children are being taught there is no Truth, that everything is relative, and that there are no moral absolutes.

* I've been appalled by the offensive TV programs being produced...and by the number of Christians who regularly watch ungodly content.

* I've been outraged that our public schools can teach our children about Islam, have them chant Islamic prayers in school, and even have them plan a Jihad as part of their curriculum. But speak a word about Jesus Christ? Forbidden!

Perhaps what is most disturbing is how weak we, as the Church, have become. Paul wrote that *"God has not given us a spirit of timidity, but of power and love and discipline"* (2 Timothy 1:7). Yet many Christians seem enslaved to this *"spirit of timidity."* Where is the courage of David? Where is the fearless dedication of Daniel? Where is the boldness of Paul?

We've allowed the world to convince us we need to be "politically correct," and in doing so, we have let the enemy overrun us...with little protest or struggle.

Well, I for one, am fighting back! And for me, this begins by personal repentance and asking God for His forgiveness. It's time for the Body of Christ to return to serving the Lord with all our heart, soul, mind, and strength (Mark 12:30). And I'm asking you to join me.

MUCH IS REQUIRED

There are many people and organizations today determined to eliminate God, Christianity, and righteousness from our national life.

Will they win? Will they continue to re-make America into a non-Christian nation? Will they wipe out our spiritual history? Will we allow judges to place even more obstacles in front of our churches and belittle our Christian witness? Will our God-based principles continue to be removed from our schools, businesses, and public life? Will our media remain a cesspool that fills our homes with filth and immorality?

While the outcome of our nation hangs in the balance, there are some questions *you* must answer:

* Will you humble yourself, seek the Lord, repent, and turn from your wicked ways? (2 Chronicles 7:14)

* Will you be silent and passive, and let the enemy win a mighty battle or will you choose to speak out against the unrighteousness sweeping across our country?

* Will you allow godlessness to grow until God is forced to bring His judgment on us or will you return to following the Lord with your whole heart and intercede for this nation?

* What will you personally do to improve the moral condition of our country?

* How seriously will you take your responsibility as a Christian American?

While some Believers resignedly quote the old hymn that says, "This world is not my home, I'm just passing through," the

Word of God makes it clear that each of us has a responsibility and a duty while we are here on earth. We are to be the *"light of the world"* and obey Jesus' clear instruction to *"let your light shine"* (Matthew 5:14-16). We also have obligations as Christians and as citizens (1 Timothy 2:1-2; 1 Peter 2:13-14).

We need to be reminded that Jesus told us, *"From everyone who has been given much, much will be required; and to whom they entrusted much, of him they will ask all the more"* (Luke 12:48). God has generously poured out His favor on each of us and on America, and in return, much is demanded of us, as a nation, and as individuals.

OUR RESPONSE

You and I will one day give an account for what we did with the time, talent, and treasure God gave us. What will we say when the Almighty judges America? That we were "just passing through?" How will we answer for the freedoms we've been given? What will be our response when we stand before God, and He asks what we did to curb the tide of sin and immorality in our own lives and in America?

> You and I will one day give an account for what we did with the time, talent, and treasure God gave us.

Every Christian needs to take this subject seriously, and every born-again Believer can make a difference. You have a responsibility to vote and let your voice be heard. If you are a follower of Jesus Christ, God is calling you today to care about our country and let your light shine. He is asking you to take a stand for righteousness, Christianity, and Biblical Truth.

As you read this book, allow your heart to be stirred by the crisis we face. Don't bury your head in the sand or assume this is not *your* battle.

In the following pages, I'll offer you both an historical *and* a Biblical perspective of America. In addition, I will present you with some alarming facts concerning the current moral condition of our nation. Although many books could be filled with all the sobering details, I only have enough space here to provide a glimpse of just how serious things have become in our country. I'll also suggest some practical things you can do.

TIME FOR AN INVENTORY

My purpose is not to shock or discourage you, but rather I am trying to warn you why this subject is so important. Candidly, our situation is grim, but not hopeless. We serve the God of the miraculous. He has performed miracle after miracle throughout our history and given us just what we needed.

But we must realize that we cannot continue down the path we're on. *Something must change.* Will we experience a mighty revival? Or will God send judgment? The choice is ours.

As a people, we must return to living according to Biblical standards and principles, and submit our lives to the Lord. In preparation for responding to this call to stand for righteousness, I'm asking you to pause now and take an inventory of your life:

* Are you truly living for God?

* Are you putting the principles and teaching of the Bible into practice in your life?

* Are you praying diligently for America?

* Do you really believe God has given you delegated authority on earth?

* Are you ready to take the spiritual offensive, even if it means leaving your "comfort zone" and taking risks?

* Are you willing to vote for candidates who know what it means to truly have a personal relationship with Jesus Christ instead of merely pandering to Christians for their vote?

This is a stand all of us must make. I need to act with boldness – and so do you. My prayer is that America will heed the call and return to righteousness...if not, we most assuredly are on the Eve of Destruction.

Americans are not voicing their displeasure loudly and frequently enough. Too many of us don't really care or are happy with the ways things are.

Chapter Two

ARE THINGS REALLY THAT BAD?

"WHAT IS DECENT?"

This question filled the cover of a recent television industry publication. Why? Because Americans had become up in arms about "indecent" television programs and demanded that something be done! So the industry was reacting to pressure from Congress and the Federal Communications Commission (FCC).

Yes, government officials will take action *if* Americans complain loudly and frequently enough. But will meaningful changes be made? I'm doubtful. Why? Because Americans are *not* voicing their displeasure loudly and frequently enough. Too many of us don't really care or are happy with the ways things are. And those of us who do complain usually are not as bold and determined as our adversaries.

Special interest groups, producers, and network executives are fighting back. To cries demanding, "Decency!" they cry back, "Censorship!" Some argue that we should not even discuss "decency."

What do these creators of indecent television really want? Freedom to do and say whatever they please. After all, isn't that the "American way"? Isn't this their "First Amendment freedom"?

They despise laws, restrictions, or rules. While they say they desire "freedom," they really just want "license" to do what they please with no responsibility or accountability to anyone.

But just imagine if people applied the same standards to driving a car! Can we envision someone saying that they wanted to be free to do whatever they felt like on our highways? Imagine if there were no speed limits, stop signs, or traffic lights! What would happen if we let any anyone drive...even children? Yes, we have the freedom to drive, but there are laws, and there are serious consequences for breaking them.

We also have rules and consequences concerning money. It's true that we're "free" to spend our money and buy "whatever" we want, but there are limits. Just imagine the chaos that would ensue if everyone – including teenagers – had unlimited credit cards and could buy whatever they wanted whenever they wanted it!

In addition, we have rules and consequences for the words we speak. Yes, we're "free" to say anything, but if we falsely scream, "Fire!" in a crowd, we're held responsible for the aftermath. And if we say the wrong thing at the wrong time, we can be sued or lose a job, a friend, or even a spouse.

It's obvious we need rules to govern the extent of our freedom. Yet some people don't understand – or choose to ignore – the need for regulations and standards regarding what is aired on television. These TV executives and producers believe they have the right to fill our networks with vile ideas and images without submitting to restrictions or limits.

Yes, we *are* free. But there are conditions to our freedom. Our liberty comes with a price, and there are consequences for our actions.

The fact that we now are forced to deal with questions about decency demonstrates just how badly things have deteriorated in this country! Our moral compass has become so confused, we can't even agree anymore on what is decent! Or if it really matters if something *is* decent!

A SPIRITUAL CONFLICT

I have seen things on television that shocked me, and I've been appalled by things that have been said in the TV industry…things I never dreamed possible! Here is just one example:

During a recent cable TV industry trade show, our Inspiration Ministries' booth was placed directly next to a booth for a network carrying "gay, lesbian, and transgender" programs into the homes of America 24 hours a day.

Were the representatives from that network embarrassed or concerned? No. They seemed delighted that others found their content offensive. They appeared defiant and determined that everyone would know what they stood for. Not that long ago, the idea of a single television program – let alone an entire network like this – would have seemed impossible. But today, it's part of our new, tragic reality.

Meanwhile, video images in their booth tantalized or revolted convention attendees with shameless content. Were they embarrassed or concerned? No. They delighted that others found their content offensive.

But what was even more disturbing was how many people stopped to listen to their message. Were they drawn by curiosity? Sympathy? Did they share the commitment to this "alternative lifestyle"? Perhaps they just were being "tolerant."

What we experienced that day was war. Not just a business or social war. It was a *spiritual* conflict inspired from the pit of hell. As Christians, networks and programs of this nature cannot help but shock us. But what we witnessed that day was just the tip of the iceberg!

When cable television burst on the scene in the 1970s, many Americans were horrified to discover they had started receiving programs filled with nudity, obscene language, and gruesome violence. And through the years, the immorality on television has grown increasingly worse.

Today, nothing seems to be off limits or taboo. Programs show or discuss just about anything, while major television cable companies and satellite providers regularly offer pornographic TV channels and homosexual programming.

"FAMILY" HOUR?

In June 2005, Viacom (the same company that owns Nickelodeon, MTV, VH1, Paramount Pictures, and other media properties) launched Logo, a network aimed at gays and lesbians. Within just one year, Logo was available in 23 million households.

During that first year, more than 60 major companies had advertised on Logo, including Dell, Eastman Kodak, eBay, General Motors, Johnson & Johnson, Sears, Sony, and Subaru. The advertising agency that works for the network commented, "There was pent-up demand for a channel to cater to this consumer."[1]

Programs on Logo included "First Comes Love," (described as "a gay-wedding reality show") and "Noah's Arc" (described as "a drama that has been likened to 'Sex and the City'" with four friends who are "gay, male, African-Americans based in Los Angeles").[2] How do Christian Americans react to programming like this?

More and more, this questionable content is spilling over into programs that used to be "family friendly." Gay characters now show up on programs airing on "family entertainment channels" during the "family" hour. Some networks even feature programs that contain openly homosexual content (such as "Boy Meets Boy" and "Queer Eye for the Straight Guy").

All this media attention has helped change the attitude of millions of Americans toward topics such as homosexuality. In a recent study, the Barna Group discovered that young adults "have amazingly unbiblical views about issues like homosexuality."

God's Word is clear about this subject. In the Law, He commanded, *"You shall not lie with a male as one lies with a female; it is an abomination"* (Leviticus 18:22). The punishment was severe: *"If there is a man who lies with a male as those who lie with a woman, both of them have committed a detestable act; they shall surely be put to death"* (Leviticus 20:13).

The Apostle Paul writes, *"Do not be deceived, neither fornicators, nor idolaters, nor adulterers, nor effeminate, nor homosexuals...will inherit the kingdom of God"* (1 Corinthians 6:9-10).

Yet God's Word and His standards on such subjects do not matter to many people. Almost half of young adults believe that "sexual relationships between people of the same sex are acceptable"! Even 25% of older adults believe this![3]

You tell *me* if you think the media has anything to do with these levels of acceptance!

WHERE ARE THE BOUNDARIES?

In the past, people were shocked when a man and women had sex outside of marriage. But now unmarried couples engaged in a sexual relationship are featured on almost every channel, just about every hour of the day. Adultery is commonplace, even in the most "wholesome" programs. So are witchcraft and the occult. Teen sex and promiscuity are encouraged. As a result, extramarital sex no longer is considered an outrage. In fact, producers now treat this as *normal*.

Over the last several decades, we've seen America increasingly reject God's standards concerning marriage and choose instead to believe the lies offered by the media. In 1969, a Gallup Poll revealed that 66% of Americans frowned on premarital sex (and just 21% felt these relations were acceptable). Contrast that with current statistics, which reveal that today "only 38% of U.S. adults say it is wrong for a man and a woman to have sexual relations before marriage." The majority of Americans (60%) now reject what the Bible says, and they have formed their own standards.[4]

In earlier times, people had enough moral conviction to avoid crass or foul language on television.

One recent study found that "seventh and ninth graders were more likely to approve of premarital sex after watching MTV for one hour." *Just one hour!* Imagine how their beliefs are being impacted as they watch this violence and sex-filled network on a daily basis!

In the past, it was considered inappropriate to talk about pornography. Yet today, prime-time programs airing on major entertainment channels openly discuss this topic. As a result, we have raised a generation who believe viewing illicit material is just another choice.

In earlier times, people had enough moral conviction to avoid crass or foul language on television. But now there are few boundaries. Words that used to be banned are now commonplace. Today's TV producers often don't bother with restraint and just cover any "offensive" words with a "bleep."

A recent study of MTV, for example, reported that within one week, there were more than 18 instances of bleeping *per hour*. And all of "these bleeped utterances were easily decipherable through context."[5]

The volume of offensive language continues to escalate. A report from the Parents Television Council (PTC) revealed that "foul language increased overall during every time slot between 1998 and 2002," including an increase of 94.8% during the "Family Hour" of 8:00-9:00 p.m. and a 109.1% increase between 9:00–10:00 p.m.[6] And there is no sign that this trend is declining!

Programs targeting teens are filled with lewd behavior and content that would horrify their parents...annual spring break specials that feature "strip-offs"...reality shows in which kids live together without supervision and engage in openly sexual activities...and even worse!

Content continues to grow increasingly provocative as producers stretch the boundaries to make their programs as sensational as possible. Nothing seems too wild or too extreme. There is no moral restraint. In fact, when a network censored one of its programs because it contained sexually explicit dialogue, the program's producer called their actions "the most chilling thing I've ever faced."[7]

DO WE REALLY CARE?

While Hollywood continues to give America more and more immorality, Americans have continued to cry out for more faith-based, family-oriented content on television. In fact, a Zogby poll in November 2006 revealed that 84% of American adults were "not offended by references to God or the Bible on network television shows." And 51% said that "entertainment networks should develop shows with positive messages and specific references to God and the Bible."

But, instead, today's media usually depicts Christians in negative and even hostile ways.

A PTC study concluded that most TV programs are "out of touch with the American public" and they "regularly portray religion in a negative light." In fact, in 2005 – 2006, "there were more negative depictions of religion than positive ones (35% to 34%)."[8]

We have not been blind to these trends. In fact, 63% of Americans "strongly agree that there is too much indecent material on television."[9]

Another PTC study revealed that compared to 1998 levels, violence on television in 2006 had increased in every time slot, including a 45% increase during the 8:00 p.m. Family Hour, a 92% increase during the 9:00 p.m. hour, and an amazing 167% increase during the 10:00 p.m. hour.[10]

But while many Americans are up in arms, others aren't so unhappy. One study reported that "most Americans aren't all that concerned" about "obscenity" in the media. Nearly

66% of adults said that cable programming should be unrestricted by the government and that basic cable networks "should be able to carry whatever programming they please." And only 30% stated that cable content is sometimes too extreme. In addition, 77% said that pay networks "should be given even greater latitude to run unrestricted fare."

What does all this mean? Even more offensive content.[11]

While many may like this "freedom," they also are quick to complain about the cultural problems that clearly are the result of this licentiousness. The fact is that TV programs rarely show the consequences of the behavior they portray or the impact on people's behavior.

A DIRECT CONNECTION

A study from the University of North Carolina revealed that "sexually charged music, magazines, TV, and movies push youngsters into intercourse at an earlier age." Researchers looked at 1,017 adolescents when they were aged 12 to 14 and again two years later.

They found that the more teens were exposed to movies, TV shows, music and magazines, the more their sexual activity increased. In fact, teens with more exposure were more than twice as likely "to have had intercourse at ages 14 to 16 than similar youngsters who had the least exposure."[12]

Numerous studies have shown how television influences behavior. Representatives of six of America's leading public health organizations, including the American Academy of Pediatrics, the American Psychological Association, and the American Medical Association, signed a statement regarding the impact of entertainment violence on children.

Their conclusion? Based on over 30 years of research and more than 1000 studies, there is a direct "connection between media violence and aggressive behavior" in children. In spite of this strong evidence, TV moguls continue to deny responsibility and go on creating an environment filled with lust, licentiousness, godlessness, and violence.

Recently, when Congress and the FCC expressed concerns about violence in the media, the National Association of Broadcasters (NAB) told the government they couldn't do anything. "You are dealing with clearly protected speech. There is no doubt that every court that has ever considered the issue [has found] descriptions of violence are fully protected speech...You have a lot of very, very difficult definitional issues. What violence is the bad violence?"[13]

So they promised no attempt would be made to initiate a change.

I could fill the pages of this book with facts about the impact of television, the effect of content, and the shocking lack of concern by today's TV networks and producers. But that's just television. It would take another book to describe the horrors that have taken place in the movie industry, even in many of our culture's most popular films.

IS HOLLYWOOD CONCERNED?

A study conducted by the University of Sydney in Australia revealed that many of the most in-demand movies "paint a consequence-free view of sex and drugs." They found "no depictions of important consequences of unprotected sex such as unwanted pregnancies, HIV, or other

STDs." The only significant effects of some films "were social embarrassment."

Many also were filled with references to drugs, and 52% of the scenes involving marijuana "showed use of the drug in a positive way." And "only a quarter of the movies were entirely free of behavior such as unprotected sex, drug use, smoking, and drinking."

Is Hollywood concerned? Not really. Adam Smith, a writer with the British film magazine *Empire* articulated a common argument when he said that it isn't Hollywood's job "to be a social or moral guardian." He called such an attitude "fiction." Paul Grainge of the Institute of Film and Television Studies at the University of Nottingham, England, concluded, "I don't think you can pinpoint Hollywood as responsible for sexual immorality. Hollywood responds to social mores as well as creates them."[14]

This is the movie capitol's excuse. Do you agree?

A QUESTION OF DECENCY

How about radio? Coast-to-coast, "shock jocks" pride themselves in being offensive. Call-in shows titillate listeners with graphic content filled with lust and subjects that focus on bizarre behavior that push the boundaries. Who's listening? Regrettably millions of Christians get caught up in this web of immorality. And only rarely does anyone seem to care about the real impact these radio personalities are having on their listeners.

Just consider Don Imus, "one of radio's original shock jocks," a member of the National Broadcasters Hall of Fame, and, according to *Time Magazine,* "one of the 25 Most Influential People in America."

What made him famous? *Time* explained, "His career took flight in the 1970s with a cocaine and vodka-fueled outrageous humor. After sobering up, he settled into a mix of highbrow talk about politics and culture, with locker room humor sprinkled in." Much of his material was "racially and sexually edgy." But, in our culture this often is "considered brilliant comment, even art."[15]

However, in March 2007, when Imus made some racist and insensitive comments about the Rutgers University women's basketball team, many advertisers suddenly became outraged and withdrew as sponsors. Were they really concerned about morality? Decency?

The fact is these advertisers routinely sponsored programs that encourage indecency, immorality, violence, homosexuality, adultery, the occult, and anti-Christian standards. They all knew about Imus' history and his often "edgy," controversial, and offensive actions; this was precisely *why* they advertised on his programs.

But two weeks after Imus made his remarks, his employers – CBS and MSNBC – feeling the heat, were compelled to fire him, primarily because of actions by his advertisers.

In pious indignation, CBS President and Chief Executive Officer Leslie Moonves commented, "There has been much discussion of the effect language like this has on our young people, particularly young women of color trying to make their way in this society. That consideration has weighed most heavily on our minds as we made our decision."

Yet this same organization had no problem for years as Imus regularly spewed other insensitive comments. But

Moonves admitted that Imus "has flourished in a culture that permits a certain level of objectionable expression that hurts and demeans a wide range of people." Yet they felt compelled to take him off the air. By taking this action he said that he believed that "we take an important and necessary step not just in solving a unique problem, but in changing that culture, which extends far beyond the walls of our company."[16]

Did Moonves really mean what he said? Was he truly serious about making changes? Solving this "unique problem"? Looking at the impact of the media on American lives? Not likely.

LYRICS AND LIFESTYLE

No wonder our country is in trouble! Will the media stop spreading a gospel of immorality? Will businesses ever consider the impact of their dollars? Will Christians ever stop supporting organizations that encourage unbiblical lifestyles?

Have you listened to the songs that dominate today's music scene? A few decades ago, radio stations were inundated with complaints when they played a song that called on listeners to "spend the night together." But today's lyrics are far more explicit using language that I wouldn't dare to repeat!

What are current artists singing about? Open sex. A promiscuous lifestyle. Murder. Death. Torture. Drugs. The occult. Hatred. And when they sing about God, it's in defiance and mockery.

In 1997, Senator Sam Brownback (R-KS) convened a series of hearings to examine "Music Violence: How Does It Affect Our Youth?"[17] His committee reported that America's youth were "in crisis" and in "more danger" than ever before. Just consider these facts:

* Though the teenage population shrank from the mid-1980s to the mid-1990s, teen arrests for murder jumped nearly 160%. Similar hikes have occurred for aggravated assault (nearly 100%), simple assault (more than 140%), and robbery (nearly 60%).

* About three million kids between 12 and 17 use marijuana, and their use has doubled since 1990. The percentage of kids in that age group using cocaine jumped 167% between 1992 and 1995. Their use of crack (up 108%) and heroin (up 92%) also soared.

* By the time they leave their teens, about 80% of males and more than 70% of females have had sex. More than 70% of births to teenagers are illegitimate. Three million teens contract a sexually transmitted disease each year.

* Teen suicide has more than tripled since 1970 and is the second leading cause of death among youth in America.

Why is all this happening? There is strong evidence to blame the music kids are listening to. "Too many people, however, have ignored the contribution made by the violent and sex-oriented messages carried by popular music, one of the most powerful cultural influences in human history."

THE EFFECT
ON BEHAVIOR

A study by the Rand Corporation revealed the tragic impact the music scene is having on our culture.[18] The study concluded that "much of popular music aimed at teens contains sexual overtones. Its influence on their behavior appears to depend on how the sex is portrayed."

Increasingly, men are depicted as "sex-driven studs" while women are seen as sex objects. "Teens who said they listened to lots of music with degrading sexual messages were almost twice as likely to start having intercourse or other sexual activities within the following two years as were teens who listened to little or no sexually degrading music. Among heavy listeners, 51% started having sex within two years, versus 29% of those who said they listened to little or no sexually degrading music."

Who is setting the standards for our kids? Just consider the music they're listening to.

A number of years ago, concern over content forced the industry to adapt a warning label to indicate content that was offensive. That strategy has backfired. Today, those warning labels are badges of honor, advertising that the music contains lyrics guaranteed to offend anyone with moral sensibilities.

With modern "monster car" audio systems, people overwhelm passing motorists with their blaring music and lyrics. On more than one occasion, while driving or stopped at a traffic light, I've been appalled at what I heard resonating from nearby cars. Perhaps you've had the same experience.

If you pay attention to these lyrics, consider that these words are being crammed into the minds of millions of impressionable young people. And we wonder why our society is in trouble. Why there is so much violence and hatred. Why so many people are confused, and so few know the Truth...or even believe there *is* a Truth.

ONE CLICK AWAY!

Then there's the Internet, where pornography and every imaginable form of wickedness are just a click away for anyone, even children. And how many individuals, including many Christians, have given in to its temptations?

You may ask me, "Are things really all *that* bad?" Just look at the world of media today and see for yourself. Yes, things are *that* bad! And they're getting worse!

Through the years, I have seen how media has shaped society – for good or bad – and how standards have changed. The media, which used to stand for morality and moral principles, largely has abandoned this commitment in favor of compromise, hedonism, lust, greed, and self-centeredness.

Why has the media become such a target for the devil? Because he knows its power.

The Apostle Paul referred to the devil as *"the prince of the power of the air, the spirit that now worked in the children of disobedience"* (Ephesians 2:2). His particular control is over *"the power of the air."*

Why would he want this power? Because the air represents the words we speak, the images we see, our thoughts, and our ideas.

And the air is the realm of the media. All forms of media.

So is it any surprise that the devil targets this domain? He knows media is the most powerful tool available today. It shapes opinions. It creates standards for behavior. It influences the way people think and act. It tells them what is true and what is false. It communicates what they should believe. It creates the social environment.

Some media representatives deny this truth. They assert they're just providing "entertainment" or offering "an escape" from the stress of everyday life. They're just "reflecting the views and behavior of society."

But if what they say is true, why do advertisers spend billions of dollars each year on commercials that influence our decisions? Why do they depend so heavily on the media to communicate fashion trends, determine election results, and tell us what to buy?

The simple fact is that millions of people are swayed by the standards set by television, Hollywood, the music industry, the Internet, and other media forms.

> **The simple fact is that millions of people are swayed by the standards set by television.**

Even many Christians allow the media to shape their attitudes. Sadly, they have become conformed to the world (Romans 12:2). Then they wonder why they seem to feel defeated, cannot experience victory in their lives, and do not have the joy of the Lord. And they question why so many young people today have abandoned the Church or adopted their own version of Christianity. Why so many don't know the Bible or understand what it teaches. Why "alternative lifestyles" have such an attraction!

WHO DEFINES CHRISTIANITY?

God wants us to realize that Satan uses media to deceive us into adopting bad habits and filling our minds with harmful thoughts and images.

In the process, Christianity has been redefined in our culture. Even though we still are considered a "Christian" nation, many politicians, media executives, and special interests groups are on an intense campaign to eradicate every indication of Christianity from our public life.

In the process, it's Christians who are described as the "extremists." When we stand up for Biblical principles, we're called "rightwing fundamentalists," and our views are dismissed as radical.

So what are today's "norms"? Many people say "normal" means a life without God. Without the Bible. Without Christianity. Without rules. There's no such thing as "right and wrong."

However, before the children of Israel entered the Promised Land, Moses warned them, *"You shall not do at all what we are doing here today, every man doing whatever is right in his own eyes"* (Deuteronomy 12:8). But that is what exists at this very moment. We're living in a culture without moral standards, with people who believe, "If it feels good, do it."

We see the devil at work throughout our country, blinding people into adapting this standard of relativism and compromise, while rejecting Truth and Biblical principles.

Yes, things *are* bad. And they're getting worse. But what is most alarming is how few Christians really are up in arms. Many Believers even seem to have bought the lies of the enemy. They've given up or given in. "We don't want to be too radical," some say. "We don't wish to offend anyone."

Sometimes, I wonder if these Christians have read their Bibles. Have they considered that Jesus said, *"I did not come to bring peace, but a sword"* (Matthew 10:34)? Have they forgotten how Paul, Peter, and John refused to compromise their convictions and stood boldly before the political and religious leaders of their day? (For example, see Acts 4 and 22.)

Perhaps the Bible seems too extreme for some Christians. Influenced by the media and other liberal trend setters, they now believe there are many ways to God.

But Jesus did not give us that choice. He said, *"I am the way, and the truth, and the life; no one comes to the Father but through Me"* (John 14:6). He is either right, or He is wrong. He is either who He claimed to be – the Son of God – or He is not. If we are His disciples and His followers, we need to obey and serve Him. He is the *only way* to come to the Father.

THE EMISSARIES OF SATAN

Today, many Christians are deceived. The Bible tells us that *"even Satan disguises himself as an angel of light. Therefore it is not surprising if his servants also disguise themselves as servants of righteousness, whose end will be according to their deeds"* (2 Corinthians 11:14-15). Jesus referred to the devil as the *"ruler of this world"* (John 12:31). His objective is to gain control over our minds and thoughts.

The emissaries of Satan are alive and active, spreading misinformation and confusion. Influencing people to abandon their faith. Promoting pornography and witchcraft, drugs and alcoholism. Preaching a gospel of "tolerance."

Just as he did with Adam and Eve, the enemy is encouraging us to reject or reinterpret God's Word. To deny Truth. To disobey Him. To go our own way. We have become so tolerant that we seem willing to tolerate hell itself.

Yes, things really *are* bad. And what are the results? Just look around and see what we are tolerating as a society.

But the devil's ways have never been God's will for His people. Our Heavenly Father always has called us to be distinct from the world and dedicated to Him, and to be on guard against the dangers of compromise.

Make no mistake: The forces that oppose Christians are strong, powerful, well-organized, and well-financed. And they are shrewd. After all, whether the agents on earth know it or not, they are managed from the pit of hell.

Some people think they have won a victory by trying to repress Christianity and eliminate spiritual influence. But what they have done is to unleash a wave of horror and deception.

For anyone with eyes to see, the evidence is clear.

People have been led to believe they are more "free" than ever before, but in reality, they are more enslaved, as we have witnessed the spreading epidemic of problems: divorce, drugs, violence, terrorism, war, and moral depravity.

Yet instead of opening our eyes and facing the Truth, and instead of seeking to return to righteousness, our country increasingly is rejecting Biblical standards as Americans are encouraged to act in any way they want without regard for practical or eternal consequences.

ARE WE PREPARED FOR THE BATTLE?

Based on what's happening around the world, things may be getting worse very soon.

Many countries are enacting "hate speech" legislation aimed at preventing anyone from saying anything that is perceived to be negative about homosexuals. Early in 2007, the

UK's Parliament enacted regulations that made it illegal for any schools in Britain to teach that homosexual conduct is immoral, including private, Christian schools! Why?

Because enough people felt that these regulations were needed to "combat discrimination against homosexuals." And almost no one raised a voice of opposition. They made it illegal to use the word "homosexual," forcing everyone – including Christians – to say that people have an "orientation toward people of the same sex."[19]

What does this mean? It is now *illegal* in the UK to preach the Gospel or even to quote the Bible on a subject such as homosexuality.

Could this happen in the United States? It is a real possibility. This kind of "hate speech" legislation has been promoted aggressively in our nation. In fact, HR Bill 1592 (which includes similar "hate speech" language) actually was being considered in Congress even as I write this book. And it may become law!

Some organizations like the American Civil Liberties Union have advocated this legislation to promote homosexuality. But this also has been inspired by organizations such as the Hindu American Foundation that wants to restrict what Christians can say about Hinduism or other religions.[20]

> Some people think they have won a victory by trying to repress Christianity and eliminate spiritual influence.

Can we imagine it being illegal in America to speak up publicly or over the airwaves about what the Bible says? No. But that is exactly what may happen. *Unless* there are changes. *Unless* Christians stand up.

Is there hope for America? Is it too late? With God, it is never too late. But as His people, we need to ask ourselves if we are ready for the battle it inevitably will take to reverse the tide of evil sweeping over our nation.

We serve a holy God who is perfectly righteous and who cannot tolerate the presence of sin. At some point, He must execute judgment. Have we reached that point in our country? Based on the evidence, we may have.

God was willing to spare Sodom and Gomorrah if only ten people living there were found to be righteous (Genesis 18:32). As long as there is even one voice crying out for change, God may hold off judgment, at least for a season.

I am adding my voice to others who are trying to awaken Christian America. Will you?

Yes, *things are bad.* We must wake up! We must take this issue seriously! We must go to war spiritually!

Chapter Three

A NATION THAT DEPENDS ON GOD

JUNE 1787 WAS A TIME OF CRISIS FOR THE Constitutional Convention in Philadelphia. Representatives of the 13 former English colonies had gathered to write a constitution. They had won their freedom in a surprising victory over the powerful English forces, but now many doubted they ever would be able to form a union. Many predicted that the states would go their separate ways.

Serious divisions remained. In particular, large and small states sharply disagreed about how they would be represented in Congress. By June 28, many felt an impasse had been reached, and a solution seemed possible. Weary and discouraged, they considered taking a break. But some felt that if they adjourned, they might never convene again, and there might never be an American nation!

At this critical hour, an elderly man rose to speak. He reminded those gathered of how they had "different sentiments on almost every question." Even though they were intelligent and well-educated, they had been "groping as it were in the dark to find political truth."

He reminded them of the nation's short history. How at the beginning of the war with England, the Continental Congress – gathered in the very room where they currently were meeting in 1787 – had asked Americans to pray for God's protection. Turning his attention to the convention chairman, George Washington, the man said, "Our prayers, Sir, were heard, and they were graciously answered." All agreed that "a Superintending Providence" had acted in their favor.

Now, they faced a new crisis. But as they had in the past, the speaker told them that the solution was to turn to God. Quoting from James 1:17, he said, "We have not hitherto once thought of humbly applying to the *'Father of lights'* to illuminate our understanding." He asked, "Have we now forgotten that powerful Friend?"

The room was packed with men whose names fill the pages of our history books. But the sage reminded them they owed their success, not to any general or army, nor to the brilliance of any thinker or the power of a political movement, but they owed everything to *God*.

Referencing the words of Jesus, he continued, "If a sparrow cannot fall to the ground without his notice, is it probable that an empire can rise without His aid?" And he quoted David from Psalm 127: "We have been assured, Sir, in the sacred writings that *'except the Lord build they labor in vain that build it.'*" There was no doubt in his mind that this was true, adding, "I firmly believe this."

He knew that the country could not have won its independence without God's help. And now they had to depend on the Lord to build this American "house." They could not form a nation, or survive, without Him: "I also believe that without His concurring aid, we shall succeed in this political building no better than the builders of Babel."

It was God who gave them unity and hope. It was the Almighty who would provide the strength and wisdom they needed, and who would be their Shield and Defender, their Guide and Help.

The man speaking also told them that without God's intervention, "we shall be divided by our little partial local interests; our projects will be confounded, and we ourselves shall become a reproach and a bye word down to future age."

At this hour of crisis, he proposed a solution. What was his answer? Prayer.

He challenged them that "prayers imploring the assistance of Heaven, and its blessings on our deliberations, be held in this Assembly every morning before we proceed to business."

Who was this man? A pastor? Church leader? A theologian? No. This was *Benjamin Franklin*. Scientist. Inventor. Writer. Businessman. Publisher. And a man known for being skeptical about religion. Yet here he was, shortly before his death, declaring openly that their key to success was their faith in God.

In spite of doubts and questions earlier in his life, Franklin had come to realize that America could not succeed without God and that our national life needed to be based on Biblical principles. He had no reservations about quoting from the Bible, and he realized their only hope was to turn to God...to seek Him and ask for His help and wisdom.

A MIRACLE HAD TAKEN PLACE

The situation in Philadelphia that summer was critical. But in the end these men created the United States Constitution

When they looked back in the years that followed, they all seemed to fully grasp that a miracle had taken place.[21]

Today, we may not realize it, but we live in a country whose very creation was a miracle! God answered prayers in powerful ways.

The words Franklin spoke in Philadelphia in 1787 still ring true today. In our time, we face a crisis. A crisis about the future and even the very survival of our country.

As He did in 1787, God *cares* about America. Franklin reminded those delegates that God sees every sparrow that falls. He also knows the number of the hairs on our head (Matthew 10:29-31).

God has an interest in who governs this nation and in our elections and elected officials. He is the One who raises up leaders and sets down others (1 Samuel 2:6-10). He knows that power doesn't come from the east or the west but from *Him* (Psalm 75:5-6).

He cares about our courts and laws, our churches and families, our schools and businesses. And He cares passionately about the moral conduct of our people.

But God is concerned about America for another reason. Throughout our history, we have been a beacon for the Christian faith. More than any other nation, we have sent out missionaries and devoted our energies and resources to spreading the Gospel. An America with a weakened commitment to Christianity means more Souls will go into eternity without hearing the name of Jesus.

A NATION "UNDER GOD"?

It is clear from the earliest days of our nation that America has a unique, God-given destiny. But today our country faces a new crisis, and the way we respond to it will determine our future.

Just as the world watched back in 1787, it is watching how we will respond. The stakes are just as high today as when Benjamin Franklin stood before those delegates. Maybe they are higher!

Our coins still bear the inscription "In God We Trust," and our pledge of allegiance still says we are a nation "under God." But many want all references to God eliminated. Our Presidents still repeat the oath of office with their hands on the Bible. But for how long? In fact, a Congressman recently was sworn into office by taking his oath on the Koran and not the Bible! The Ten Commandments have been removed from our government buildings, and our children no longer can pray out loud in school.

How far will we fall? What other freedoms will we lose?

> The stakes are just as high today as when Benjamin Franklin stood before those delegates.

I really wonder if it is possible to reverse the tide: Will we continue to abandon our Biblical foundations? Will our Christian faith be squeezed completely out of our public life? Will more laws be passed that condone behavior that is offensive and displeases God?

But don't just let me tell you what *I* think. Ask yourself if you agree with what you're reading in this book. What is God saying to your spirit regarding the times in which we live? Are you concerned? If you have eyes to see and ears to hear, I believe you must be!

Some today believe the battle is already lost. That the mountain we face is too high and the obstacles before us too great. That the enemy is too strong, too rich, too well-organized.

It is true that our challenges are enormous. From a human perspective, our situation certainly looks grim.

But we serve the same God who spoke worlds into being with just a word, who could send just one angel and strike 185,000 of the Israelites Assyrian adversaries (2 Kings 19:35). He is the same God who promised that with Him, *nothing* is impossible (Luke 1:37)…who has sent revivals throughout history, often in the most unlikely places…who has intervened in seemingly hopeless situations to alter the course of nations.

Our God has not changed! And the Bible tells us that He never will (Malachi 3:6). He is the same God who…

* called brave men and women to come to these shores.

* brought about an improbable victory in our Revolutionary War.

* gave supernatural wisdom to delegates in Philadelphia and helped them create a Constitution that has been called one of the marvels of human history.[22]

* brought us through a bloody Civil War, and preserved and protected us through times of economic, social, political, and military disasters.

WHAT WILL YOUR CHILDREN SAY?

Are you willing to believe with me that God can perform miracles today? To believe that God can change the course of our nation and pour out His Spirit on us as never before? Are you willing to believe that God wants us, as a people, to return to righteousness? Are you willing to pray and to put your faith into action?

I am calling on Believers across America to return to righteousness. But that rallying call starts with each of us. We need to be like those first Pilgrims and Patriots who refused to compromise and stood determined to do what they believed was right...who were willing to fight and give their lives that *we* might be free.

You enjoy this freedom. But consider your children and grandchildren. What will *they* say about you when they look back at *your* life in the years to come? Will they testify that you took a stand for righteousness, and, like our forefathers and foremothers, stood determined to defend what you believed was right? Will you fight that *your* children and grandchildren will also be free?

Let your journey begin with this book. With God's help, if Believers will humble themselves, repent before God, and return to righteousness, there may still be hope for America, and God will pull us back from the Eve of Destruction.

We cannot forget that
one of the very first acts
by permanent English
settlers was to conduct
a public prayer meeting
and claim the land for
England and for
Christianity.

Chapter Four

GOD CHOOSES AMERICA

AMERICA HAS A HISTORY AND A HERITAGE, NOT just as a "religious" nation but also as a nation that was built on Biblical Christianity. That dedication was clear in the life and calling of Christopher Columbus, the man who "discovered" America. His name means "Christ-bearer," and that was his drive and passion.

Columbus saw the hand of God shaping his life. He was a man of prayer and sensed the Creator guiding his steps. He believed God gave him the ideas that led to the discovery of America. "It was the Lord who put into my mind (I could feel His hand upon me) the fact that it would be possible."

He knew the Bible and was sensitive to the work of the Holy Spirit. While others laughed and ridiculed his plans, he persisted, partly because there was "no question" to Columbus that his "inspiration was from the Holy Spirit." How did he know? "Because He comforted me with rays of marvelous illumination from the Holy Scriptures." He also believed he was fulfilling prophecy.[23]

God uniquely prepared Columbus and gave him "the spirit and the intelligence for the task: seafaring, astronomy, geometry, arithmetic, skill in drafting spherical maps and placing correctly the cities, rivers, mountains and ports."

At the time of Columbus' voyage, Spain recently had expelled the Muslim Moors, and many felt that "Islam was approaching its final apocalyptic battle with Christianity." Columbus was convinced God had called him to be a warrior in this battle.

On April 30, 1492, Columbus wrote Spain's King Ferdinand and Queen Isabella, "I plead with Your Majesties to spend all the treasure from this enterprise on the conquest of Jerusalem." Columbus convinced the queen that "if she would fund his adventure, he would contribute its profits to fund a glorious new crusade to the Holy Land to wrest the holy Christian sites from the infidel."[24]

Columbus set out on his journey motivated to spread the Gospel and change the course of history. As he met native peoples in the New World, he felt his highest obligation was "the conversion of these people to the holy faith of Christ."

Returning in triumph from his first voyage, he gave God the praise: "These great and marvelous results are not to be attributed to any merit of mine but to the holy Christian faith and to the piety and religion of our sovereigns." He knew that his success was due to the blessings of "the Spirit of God."

He had prayed and sought the Lord, and was confident that "God is wont to hear the prayers of His servants who love His precepts even to the performance of apparent impossibilities."

Columbus said that thanks should be rendered "to our Lord and Savior Jesus Christ, who has granted us so great a victory and such prosperity...Let Christ rejoice on earth, as He rejoices in heaven in the prospect of the salvation of the souls of so many nations hitherto lost. Let us also rejoice, as well on account of the exaltation of our faith as on account of the increase of our temporal prosperity, of which not only Spain but all Christendom will be partakers."

ZEALOUS CHRISTIANS

The explorations of Spain gradually awakened interest in the New World from other nations, including England. Some saw this opportunity as a way to gain economic, military, or political power. But many considered this as part of their Christian duty.

England's course was shaped by men like geographer Richard Hakluyt who argued that planting English colonies in America would be a "most godly and Christian work," which ultimately would lead to bringing the Gospel to the American Indians, "bringing them from darkness to light."[25]

However, the first English attempts to plant a colony failed. Many reasons have been cited for this failure, but one central reason was that this "was an entirely secular effort. It had no religious dimension." They were to learn that the key to growth and stability in America was to find Christians who would become solid citizens and work hard, and who were dependable.[26]

England did not give up its efforts to colonize North America. It divided the region into two spheres of influence. The Plymouth Company would settle an area we now know as New England, while a second group would settle near the Chesapeake Bay.

This second group was the first to depart, and 144 mariners and adventurers set out in the last days of 1606, making landfall on April 29, 1607, near the mouth of the Chesapeake Bay.

When they reached land, the first thing they did was set up a cross and name the place "Cape Henry" in honor of the oldest son of King James I. The company then gathered around Reverend Robert Hunt, who led them in a prayer of gratitude and dedication, thanking God for their safe journey and recommitting themselves to His plan and purpose for the New World.

We cannot forget that one of the very first acts by permanent English settlers was to conduct a public prayer meeting and claim the land for England and for Christianity.

It took several years for the Plymouth Company to arrange its voyage. The nucleus was drawn from a group of English men and women who had been living in Holland, exiled because of their faith in God. They had chosen to be separate from the Church of England rather than seek to reform it from within.

> We cannot forget that one of the very first acts by permanent English settlers was to conduct a public prayer meeting...

As they began thinking about immigrating to America, they had many debates. They knew their journey would be risky and dangerous. But these were radical Christians, men and women with a zealous commitment to God and His Kingdom. They understood they were taking risks, but to them, the hazards were part of their life of faith.

Ultimately, only one thing mattered to them: They knew this was what God wanted. They were following His call to settle America.

To them, this mission was part of their spiritual destiny, as well as God's plan for mankind. Their beliefs were shaped by their study of the Bible and the spiritual forces in the world. One of their leaders, William Bradford, saw how life on earth was divided into two kingdoms with two influences: the Kingdom of God and the kingdom of Satan.

He realized that life was a spiritual war and that Christians were under constant attack by Satan, who sought to spread darkness. The enemy had tried to "destroy the kingdom of Christ" by "sowing, the seeds of discord, and bitter enmity" among Christians.

A COMPACT INSPIRED BY GOD

Although the pastor of these Pilgrims, John Robinson, was not able to take the journey, his heart remained with them. He wrote several letters to encourage and guide them.

In one of these letters, written just before they sailed, he instructed them concerning their future life in the New World. This was not just a spiritual mission; they also had to think about practical things: "You are to become a body politic, using among yourselves civil government." This letter helped these Pilgrims stay on course and reminded them of their purpose for coming to America.[27]

Their ship, the Mayflower, sailed from Plymouth, England, in August 1620. It was a perilous journey. But while still at sea, the leaders gathered together and "drew up a social compact, designed to secure unity and provide for future government." This became known as the "Mayflower Compact," one of the most important documents in American history. This compact drew its inspiration from God's Covenant with Israel in the Bible.

This is significant to understand: *The first government in America was based on Christian principles and the Word of God.* In fact, God's laws became the foundation for conduct and for the government in America. There was no "separation between church and state."

The Mayflower Compact was written "in the name of God." Nothing was more important to the early Pilgrims than establishing and maintaining His Presence in their lives. They stated that they had undertaken this voyage "for the Glory of God, and Advancement of the Christian Faith."[28]

Finally, after 66 days at sea, they landed November 21 on Cape Cod at what is now Provincetown, Massachusetts, and the day after Christmas, these 102 Pilgrims arrived at the nearby site of Plymouth.

The first thing they did when their feet touched dry ground was to fall on their knees and bless God. They knew that He "had brought them over the vast and furious ocean, and delivered them from all the perils and miseries thereof, again to set their feet on the firm and stable earth, their proper element."[29]

DEPENDING ON THE ALMIGHTY

In his account of those early years, William Bradford described how they followed the example of the children of Israel when they faced trials by crying to the Lord, who heard their voice and met their needs in miraculous ways.

These early Pilgrims recognized their obligation to seek to live a righteous life. They knew God was holy and that they had to remember His laws. So they sought to maintain Godly standards. But they also recognized they were still under spiritual attack.

Even as more settlers arrived in the New World, they retained their commitment to God. The First Charter of Massachusetts on March 4, 1629, stated that they knew the reason for their success "cannot but chiefly depend [on] the Blessing of Almighty God."

Yet they still faced countless challenges and needed spiritual reinforcements. In 1630, a group under the leadership of John Winthrop arrived. Historian Paul Johnson called this "the turning-point in the history of New England" and Winthrop "the first great American."

Winthrop believed that only a commitment to God and His Kingdom would enable them to survive. He was very conscious of their influence on the world and knew that people back in England and throughout Europe were watching what they did. Even while on board the ship en route to America, he reminded them, "We must consider that we shall be as a City upon a Hill, the eyes of all people are upon us."[30]

He was right. People everywhere began looking to see what was happening in the New World. But even from the beginning, everyone knew that America was a Christian nation.

It's also vital to note that when Columbus, Hunt, Bradford, Winthrop, and the early settlers came to this new America, along with all of our founding fathers who spoke of "God," they were referring to the God of the Bible. They weren't speaking of Allah, Buddha, or some other religion that claimed to have a "god." They were calling upon the God of Abraham, Isaac, and Jacob. They were calling upon the God and Father of our Lord Jesus Christ, the one true God, the Lord, the I Am!

Because they were
so conscious of the
holiness of God, they
wanted to rid their life
of sin and anything that
displeased Him.

Chapter Five

A CHRISTIAN NATION

AMERICANS NEVER HAVE BEEN PERFECT PEOPLE. Even the most spiritual and reverent Pilgrims still were sinners saved by grace. Yet consistently throughout our history, God has moved upon us by His mighty hand to bring us back to our knees. To humble us. To keep us focused on Him. To remind us of our destiny as a Christian nation.

The first great move of God in this country took place in the early 18th century. Known as "the Great Awakening," this has been called "one of the key events in American history." No one knows for sure when or how it began, but it seems to have been started by German or Dutch immigrants who were grateful to have found freedom in America.

Their spirit of thanksgiving brought a new focus on God. Revival was sparked in 1719 when Theodore Frelinghuysen led a series of meetings in the Raritan Valley in New Jersey. This revival was born out of a concern for "Pietism." Because they were so conscious of the holiness of God, they wanted to rid their life of sin and anything that displeased Him. These were humble people who were hungry for Him.

THE "LOG COLLEGE"

As Americans started pushing westward, the revival spread. One of the key people in this move of God was William Tennent, a Scotch-Irish Presbyterian, who settled at Neshaminy, Pennsylvania, in the 1720s. There he built his "Log College," where he taught many students who became preachers and brought the Gospel throughout the colonies. His college became the prototype for the institutes of higher learning in America, inspiring for example, the College of New Jersey, which eventually became known as Princeton University.[31]

As word about this revival became known, others wanted to learn more. They began asking what God was saying to His people. They became less satisfied with the things of this world and hungered for more of Him.

One of those men was Jonathan Edwards, called by an historian "a man of outstanding intellect and sensibility" and "the first major thinker in American history."[32]

Revival broke out, and the spiritual awakening spread.

As pastor of the Congregationalist church in Northampton, Massachusetts, Edwards was concerned about the spiritual life of his church. In 1734 he began a series of sermons on "Justification by Faith Alone." He called people to seek God and not trust in their religious activities, to repent and turn from their worldliness and wickedness.

Under Edwards' powerful preaching, men and women began confessing their sins. Suddenly they became conscious of God's holiness and realized how much they needed Him. They began seeking to become right with Him and started praying with more intensity.

Their faith became the most treasured thing in their lives, and people even closed their businesses to spend more time seeking the Lord and hearing His Word proclaimed.

"I THIRST!"

Revival broke out, and the spiritual awakening spread, continuing to expand and reaching a new crest in 1735 when 25-year-old George Whitefield arrived from England. Whitefield was the illegitimate son of an English barmaid, yet God used him powerfully to spread the Gospel throughout England and America.

The turning point in his life came when a minister directed him to the message of Jesus: *"If any man thirst, let him come unto me, and drink. He that believeth on me, as the scripture hath said, out of his belly shall flow rivers of living water"* (John 7:37-38 KJV). When he read these verses, Whitefield cried aloud, "I thirst!" This thirst for God led him to a life of ministry and service.

Whitefield brought that message to America in seven missionary visits. Tens of thousands of people realized they, too, thirsted for God. In one 75-day period, he preached 175 times and traveled 800 miles, a staggering distance in that era.

With a voice that was described as "riveting," he could be heard long distances away. Whitefield's message was that everyone needed to be born again. He preached in meeting houses, barns, fields, and from wagons. After delivering his message, he would wait for the Spirit to move.[33]

And the Spirit did move time after time, bringing conviction and repentance as people responded by crying out for God.

Whitefield's influence spread throughout society, even to political and business leaders. Benjamin Franklin wrote, "It was wonderful to see the change made by his preaching in the manners of the inhabitants of Philadelphia. From being thoughtless or indifferent about religion, it seemed as if the whole world were growing religious."

As revival swept through the land, others joined in the crusade. Another prominent preacher was John Davenport. He also called on people to rid their lives of worldliness and wickedness. The civil authorities reacted to his methods, and he was arrested, tried, and judged to be mentally disturbed. But that did not stop him or others who were called to preach. Denied pulpits in churches, Davenport and other preachers spoke in the open, often around campfires.

SETTING THE TONE

The impact of the "Great Awakening" throughout the colonies was enormous. People renounced a worldly lifestyle and craved to live a holy life and draw closer to God, impacting every denomination and region of the country.

This revival continued for more than 40 years until *after* 1760. It was estimated that as many as 50,000 people gave their hearts to the Lord, and hundreds of churches were founded.[34]

But as so often has happened throughout history, this move of God was resisted by the religious establishment. Yet no one today, not even the most cynical atheist, can deny how the Great Awakening stirred and shaped our society. However, what is perhaps most significant is how this revival set the tone for America society, including the most important moments in our history: our War of Independence and the formation of the American government.

This revival changed the very character of America. God had prepared the way for independence by refining our people. By calling them to prayer. By reminding them to repent of their sins. By encouraging righteousness, and by stirring a hunger to know His Word.

As we read the history of great events like the Revolutionary War, the writing of the Declaration of Independence, and the meetings of the Continental Congress, we can never forget that behind every battle, every meeting, every decision, and every leader was a culture saturated with Christianity and a belief in the God of the Bible. Everyone knew and quoted from the Scriptures. America was a country formed by men and women who were inspired by their faith.

America was a Christian nation.

America's Founding
Fathers knew the
answer: God's sovereign
hand. They had strong
Biblical beliefs and
an intimate knowledge
of the Bible.

Chapter Six

THE CHOICES OF OUR FOREFATHERS

HOW DID AMERICA WIN ITS WAR FOR INDEPENDENCE? How were these 13 former colonies able to reach an agreement on a Constitution and form a government that would stand the test of time?

America's Founding Fathers knew the answer: God's sovereign hand.

They understood this because they shared a Christian heritage. They had strong Biblical beliefs and an intimate knowledge of the Bible. They also knew that God answers prayer. They had seen how He could work in the lives of men and women through the revivals that swept America in the 18th century.

In his analysis of our nation's early years, distinguished historian Robert Middlekauff has written, "More than anything else in America, religion shaped culture." He saw how a common culture had developed based on Christian beliefs "which held them together in the crisis of upheaval and war." Yes, there were differences, but "beneath the surface their similarities were even more striking."

But as Middlekauff observed, "The generation that made the Revolution were the children of the twice-born, the heirs of this seventeenth-century religious tradition." America's Founding Fathers acted like "men who felt that Providence had set them apart for great purposes." It was their religious belief that "gave the Revolution much of its intensity and much of its idealism."[35]

Paul Johnson explains how the religious climate in America brought unity and a sense of destiny that was fueled in large part by the Great Awakening. "The Revolution could not have taken place without this religious background."

While the French Revolution of 1789 was "an anti-religious event," America's Revolution was in its origins "a religious event. That fact was to shape the American Revolution from start to finish and determine the nature of the independent state it brought into being."

Americans drew strength and motivation from Revelation 21:5, where Jesus said, *"Behold, I make all things new."* Our Founding Fathers were conscious that they were creating something new and that God was their guiding force.[36]

THEIR SOURCE
OF INSPIRATION

Even the most skeptical and doubtful Founding Father was committed to Christianity. In 1785, for example, James Madison introduced in the Virginia House of Delegates five bills touching upon religion which Thomas Jefferson likely had drafted.[37]

These men were descended from families that had come to America for religious freedom, and they were determined that Americans not become caught up in the persecution and bloody wars that had marked European history.

But did this mean limiting or repressing religion? No. They simply were adamant that America would not have an official state church. They did not want laws that required specific religious behavior, certain beliefs, and certain activities.

These were men who grew up in the shadow of the Great Awakening. The Bible and Christianity were everywhere and formed the foundation for thought.

Where did these Founding Fathers turn for inspiration? More than any other book or person, they depended on the Bible.

The University of Houston recently conducted a ten-year study which reviewed more than 15,000 documents of all kinds written by the Founding Fathers – laws and letters, speeches and articles. The people they cited the most were Charles de Montesquieu, Sir William Blackstone, and John Locke. But the researchers were amazed to discover that more than a third of all the quotes from our Founding Fathers were *directly* from the Bible.[38]

These men knew the Scriptures and based their ideas and actions on Biblical concepts. They also knew the consequences of turning away from their faith in God.

IT STARTED WITH WASHINGTON

When we look at the lives of our Founding Fathers, we see men and women filled with love for God and committed to Biblical principles, starting with the "father" of our country, George Washington.

Washington was acutely aware of God's blessings and how much he and America depended upon Him for their very existence. He had grown up in the Church and frequently attended services. It has been said that it was his "habit to begin and close each day with a time of prayer, alone in his room."[39]

As commander of the American forces during the Revolutionary War, he and his men experienced miracle after miracle. Horses were shot out from under him but he survived unscathed. His troops were spared when they should have been wiped out. Again and again, God miraculously provided for their needs.

Washington set the tone for all the Presidents who have followed, making sure that faith in God was central to the highest office of the nation.

As leader of his army, he insisted on regular times of prayer and demanded that everyone participate. "He often warned that they could not expect the favor of God's help in their cause unless they lived in a way worthy of it. He even exhorted them to fight as true Christian soldiers. Their desperate need for the help of Providence was his constant, insistent theme."[40]

He set the tone for American military leaders, who, following his example, recognized the need for God's protection and wisdom, and frequently called out for His intervention in their battles and strategies.

As our first President, Washington also set the tone for all the Presidents who have followed, making sure that faith in God was central to the highest office of the nation.

Taking the oath of office in 1789, he laid his hands on the Bible. After repeating the short phrase required by the Constitution, he added this phrase, "So help me, God." This became a tradition carried out by all Presidents since.

Washington was very conscious of the fact that he was setting precedents other Presidents would follow. His actions in citing God and showing his dependence on the Bible were deliberate.

In his first inaugural address in 1789, Washington said, "It would be peculiarly improper to omit, in this first official act, my fervent supplications to that Almighty Being who rules over the universe, who presides in the councils of nations, and whose providential aids can supply every human defect, that His benediction may consecrate to the liberties and happiness of the people of the United States, a government instituted by themselves for these essential purposes."

He knew what obstacles America had overcome to achieve independence, and he was quick to acknowledge the hand of God. "No people can be bound to acknowledge and adore the Invisible Hand which conducts the affairs of men more than the people of the United States. Every step by which they have advanced to the character of an independent nation seems to have been distinguished by some token of Providential agency."[41]

And while Washington sometimes referred to God as "Providence," he quite clearly was referring to the God of the Bible, who he firmly believed heard and answered the prayers of His people.

ADAMS AND THE ALMIGHTY

John Adams was America's second President and first Vice President. He was a devout Christian who frequently quoted the Bible and referred to God in his speeches and letters. He believed that the signing of the Declaration of

Independence "ought to be commemorated as the day of deliverance, by solemn acts of devotion to God Almighty."

Adams knew God was America's only hope. In September 1776, he was asked if he thought the new nation would succeed in its struggle against Great Britain. His answer? "Yes, if we fear God and repent of our sins."

Where did Adams turn for wisdom? He often looked to the Bible. He once wrote Thomas Jefferson that "the Bible is the best book in the World."[42]

Adams was acutely aware that America's very life depended on God's continuing help. On August 2, 1820, he wrote Charles Carroll, "The American Union will last as long as God pleases. It is the duty of every American Citizen to exert his utmost abilities and endeavors to preserve it as long as possible and to pray with submission to Providence 'esto perpetua.'"[43]

THE FAITH OF JEFFERSON

Perhaps no one has attracted more attention as a critic of Christianity than our third President, Thomas Jefferson. He had a scientific mind and naturally questioned everything. He also was highly influenced by the French Revolution and its views against organized religion.

Jefferson might have had doubts and personal opinions, yet he stated clearly, "I am a real Christian, that is to say, a disciple of the doctrines of Jesus Christ." And he knew how much America depended upon God. In his discourse, "A Summary View of the Rights of British America" in July 1774, he wrote, "The God who gave us life gave us liberty at the same time."

In his second Inaugural Address, he told America how much he and the nation relied on God: "I shall need, too, the favor of that Being in whose hands we are, who led our fathers, as Israel of old, from their native land and planted them in a country flowing with all the necessaries and comforts of life."

He knew that God had "covered our infancy with His providence and our riper years with His wisdom and power." And he asked Americans to join him in praying "that He will so enlighten the minds of your servants, guide their councils, and prosper their measures that whatsoever they do shall result in your good, and shall secure to you the peace, friendship, and approbation of all nations."

Jefferson thought it was foolish to deny the Presence of God. In a letter he wrote to John Adams in 1823, he said that "when we take a view of the universe, in its parts, general or particular, it is impossible for the human mind not to perceive and feel a conviction of design, consummate skill, and indefinite power in every atom of its composition."

And, as he thought about the future of our country (and particularly the problem with slavery), he wrote, "I tremble for my country when I reflect that God is just; and that His justice cannot sleep forever...an exchange of situation is among possible events; that it may become probable by supernatural interference."[44]

MADISON KNEW THE MASTER

James Madison was our fourth President but also the man largely responsible for the Constitution. He "was influenced by his early training under Scots-Presbyterian Donald Robertson, to whom Madison gave credit for 'all that I have been in life.'" Madison later trained in theology at Princeton under Reverend John Witherspoon. Many of his ideas for the Constitution came from his study of the concept of Covenant in the Bible.[45]

In 1778, in the midst of the Revolutionary War, he declared, "We have staked the whole future of American civilization, not upon the power of government," but rather it was based on "the capacity of mankind for self-government" and our ability "to sustain ourselves according to the Ten Commandments."

As he began to lobby for principles that would govern the Constitution, Madison wrote that "religion [is] the basis and Foundation of Government." He knew this nation needed to depend on the Almighty: "The belief in a God All Powerful, wise and good, is so essential to the moral order of the World and to the happiness of man, that arguments which enforce it cannot be drawn from too many sources."

GODLY SIGNERS OF THE DECLARATION

We often concentrate on these first Presidents of our country and other more celebrated people. But history tells us that America was blessed with many Founding Fathers who were God-fearing, Bible-believing men. In fact, the Declaration of Independence and the Constitution of our country were written and signed by those committed to the Gospel. Did they depend upon God? Read these words of wisdom from just a few of these outstanding individuals:

* Popular and influential doctor, **Benjamin Rush**, declared openly, *"My only hope of salvation is in the infinite, transcendent love of God manifested to the world by the death of His Son upon the cross. Nothing but His blood will wash away my sins. I rely exclusively on it. Come, Lord Jesus! Come quickly!"*

* **Charles Carroll**, an influential Catholic leader from Maryland, told his son: *"I earnestly, advise you…never rise or go to bed without humbling yourself in fervent prayer before your God, and crave His all powerful grace."*

* **Samuel Chase** also was from Maryland and was a member of the Continental Congress and later an associate justice in the U.S. Supreme Court. He wrote that Christianity was our *"established religion."*

* Born in Scotland, **John Witherspoon** was president of the College of New Jersey and represented that state. He said without compromise, *"I shall now entreat…you in the most earnest manner to believe in Jesus Christ, for 'there is no salvation in any other.'"* He knew the consequences of life without Him: *"[If] you are not clothed with the spotless robe of His righteousness, you must forever perish."*

* **John Dickinson** lived *"one of the most extraordinary political lives of all of the Founding Fathers,"* representing Pennsylvania.[46] He, too, recognized the importance of the Bible: *"The Holy Scriptures are able to make us wise unto Salvation, through Faith which is in Jesus Christ."* He knew that America needed to stay true to Biblical truth and would be judged if disobedient. He wrote, *"In order to encourage us to Obedience, and to deter us from*

Disobedience, hath not God been graciously pleased to reveal, that there will be a Day of Judgment, in which He will by Jesus Christ our Lord judge all Mankind."[47]

* **Roger Sherman** was a highly respected lawyer who represented Connecticut. He declared openly his belief in the fundamental truths of Christianity: *"I believe that there is one only living and true God, existing in three persons, the Father, the Son, and the Holy Spirit...That the Scriptures of the old and new testaments are a revelation from God and a complete rule to direct us how we may glorify and enjoy Him."*

* Virginia's **Patrick Henry** provided major inspiration for our independence with his cry, *"Give me liberty or give me death."* But he also was vocal about our Christian heritage and foundation. He once said, *"It cannot be emphasized too strongly or too often that this great nation was founded, not by religionists but by Christians, not on religions, but on the Gospel of Jesus Christ."*

THE SOUND OF LIBERTY

Did this Christian foundation mean that those with other beliefs would be persecuted? No. As Patrick Henry stated, "For this very reason, people of other faiths have been afforded asylum, prosperity, and freedom of worship here."

And what sound celebrated our freedoms? It was our "liberty bell," a bell commissioned in 1751 by the Pennsylvania Assembly for its State House. Isaac Norris, the Assembly Speaker, instructed that this bell should have an inscription based on Leviticus 25:10: "Proclaim Liberty thro' all the Land to all the Inhabitants thereof."

From the moment it arrived in Philadelphia in 1753, this bell played a special role. Every time it rang, people had an opportunity to remember the inscribed Bible verse that proclaimed liberty throughout the land. The Liberty Bell symbolized both our nation's commitment to freedom and our dependence on God.

I could go on and on about our Founding Fathers. Were they perfect? No. Many had doubts and all had personal opinions. But these men were united in a belief in God. They realized they had been called by Him and that America had a special destiny.

> **Many God-fearing, Bible-believing patriots died that we might be free.**

But they also knew they had a responsibility to be good citizens. They were willing to sacrifice their time and resources, and even risk their lives. Many God-fearing, Bible-believing patriots died that we might be free. They knew that we, as a people, needed to depend upon God, and they literally gave their lives to make this freedom possible.

All of these men and women knew their forefathers came to America for religious freedom. They were Believers who wanted the right to worship God with a clear faith, belief, and love for Christ.

Their Christian, Bible-based beliefs influenced their lives and provided the foundation for this country. The legacy they left is one they never expected would change.

But today, something unbelievable has happened. Many people want to ignore the facts, re-write history, and remove God from our national life. They want to erase any mention of God and His Word from our history and deny the Christian origins of our nation. They want to ignore the truths that were obvious to George Washington, John Adams, Thomas Jefferson, James Madison, and our other Founding Fathers.

The argument frequently is made that these men primarily were "deists" and not really Christians. But this argument does not hold water.

By definition, deists believe there is a "god" but that he is not involved in the affairs of this world.[48] Some Founding Fathers were deists, but most were not, and as a group, they did not act like deists. They believed in the God of the Bible and prayed frequently – as individuals, in churches, and in public gatherings. They often called on all Americans for times of prayer and even fasting. They openly sought God's intervention.

Today, we suffer the consequences of doing what none of our Forefathers would have believed possible. Instead of calling on God, we are trying to eliminate and ignore Him. Instead of acknowledging our need of Him, we are trying to make it illegal even to mention His name.

Our Founding Fathers made their choices. We must make ours...

VISITATIONS FROM GOD

THROUGHOUT OUR HISTORY AS A NATION, THERE have been times when we have drifted away from God. We've gone through periods when our faith has grown cold. Yet no one can deny the remarkable fact that over and over again, God has intervened in the life of our country and demonstrated that we have a special destiny and mission. He cares about America, and through the centuries, He has answered her people when we have cried out to Him.

Regretfully, we consistently have followed the pattern established by the nation of Israel. In the Bible, we read how Israel often turned to God in times of crisis, only to drift away from Him when everything seemed to be going well. This has been true of America as well.

We see this pattern begin during the years following our government's formation. A spirit of complacency and coldness seemed to descend as the fires of revival faded.

The country began to be divided by rivalries, region, and political philosophy. As Americans began to move west, the rule of law often was replaced by a spirit of lawlessness. Nationwide, church attendance decreased.

But God had not forgotten about America, so He sent another wave of revival.

One of His instruments was Francis Asbury.[49] Born in Staffordshire, England, in 1745, Asbury was a man of prayer. He developed the habit of rising at 4:00 a.m. each morning to seek God, and he continued this practice his whole life.

Because of his zeal, he attracted the attention of John Wesley, who was burdened for the needs in America. In a service in 1771, Wesley challenged his congregation to give their lives to missions. In those days, *America* was the mission field!

He asked "Who will go?" Asbury answered the call, and later that year left for this new land. Why was he leaving his home for the unknown of America? He wrote in his journal that he was determined "to live to God," and he was driven that others, too, would live for Him.

He based his first sermon in America on Paul's warning, *"Let us not sleep as others do, but let us be alert and sober"* (1 Thessalonians 5:6). He felt that many were content to live in comfort with no concern for the Lost. He believed his call from God was to "spread scriptural holiness to every city and hamlet in America." He called Christians to take action and commit themselves to the Gospel.

He sought men who shared his passion for evangelism and recruited them to be circuit rider preachers. This was a hard life, and many died while still young. But they reached thousands with the Gospel, following Asbury's exhortation: "We must reach every section of America – especially the new frontiers. We must not be afraid of men, devils, wild animals, or disease. Our motto must always be FORWARD!"

Asbury called all Christians to share this commitment to advance the Gospel. In his journal, Asbury wrote, "How I wish to spend all my time and talents for Him who spilt His blood for me." Others might worry or be afraid, but Asbury was bold and fearless. He also wrote, "I have nothing to seek but the glory of God; and nothing to fear but His displeasure."

Asbury tirelessly traveled the length of America on horseback, crossing the Allegheny Mountains 60 times. Without shelter or home, he rode on rocky paths and muddy roads, often threatened by robbers and thieves. When plagued by nagging illnesses, he continued to press on, even when he was hungry or ill.

It has been said that when Asbury arrived in America, there were 1,160 Methodists. But when he died, there were 214,235. He had ordained more than 3,000 ministers and preached more than 7,000 sermons. What an amazing impact!

By 1815, Asbury was thought by many people to be "the best-known person in America." He had transformed this new nation with his zeal for God and commitment to evangelism.

One of the important strategies Asbury developed was the "camp meeting."

"HUNDREDS FELL PROSTRATE"

The first recorded, interdenominational camp meeting in America was held at Cane Ridge in Kentucky in 1801. Attended by as many as 25,000 people from all denominations, it was reported that during this meeting "hundreds fell prostrate under the mighty power of God."[50]

This and other camp meetings sparked another wave of revivals. By 1821, nearly a thousand camp meetings were being held each year among the Methodists alone.

God had answered the cries of His people, and the impact was felt throughout the growing nation. This revival set the tone for the westward advancement across the continent. Many western settlements had been known for drunkenness and immorality, but when God sent revival, lives changed. The frontier eventually became known for morality and Christian beliefs, with one traveler remarking that Kentucky had become "the most moral place I had ever seen."[51]

This spirit of revival changed the nation in many other ways. It produced a strong interest in world missions, including the formation of several important mission boards and societies. These revivals also inspired a great hunger for the Word of God and led to the formation of the American Bible Society. Revivals also ignited the growth of the Sunday school movement and the fight against slavery.

These revivals inspired a great hunger for the Word of God. Revivals also ignited the growth of the Sunday school movement and the fight against slavery.

While revival was coming to the frontier of America, it also was felt at an unusual place: Yale College in Connecticut, where a spiritual outpouring "shook the institution to its center."

Once again, God used a specially prepared man to spark this revival at the college. Timothy Dwight, grandson of Jonathan Edwards. When Dwight became president in 1795, most of the students were hostile toward Christianity. But he required them to grapple with the question, "Is the Bible the Word of God?" He led them to re-examine the principles of the Bible and the claims of Christianity.[52]

Dwight also preached a series of sermons in the college chapel. "Most devastating was the 1796 Baccalaureate sermon on 'The Nature and Danger of Infidel Philosophy.'" The effect was immediate. "From that moment infidelity was not only without a stronghold," wrote a student, "but without a lurking place. To espouse her cause was now as unpopular as before it had been to profess a belief in Christianity."

THE POWER OF BELIEVING PRAYER

The next wave of revival soon broke out under the inspiration of another intellectual, Charles Finney.[53] In addition to being a lawyer, Finney had been president of Oberlin College in Ohio. He described how he had no interest in religion but began reading the Bible because his law books contained so many references to the Mosaic Code. He became convicted and gave his heart to serve God.

He observed that "in the church I attended, I was particularly struck by the fact that the prayers I had listened to from week to week were not, that I could see, being answered." But when he read the Bible, Jesus promised that our prayers would be answered, and that if we ask, it will be given to us (Luke 11:9).

However, when people around him prayed, nothing seemed to happen: "In their prayer and conference meetings they would continually confess that they were making no progress in securing revival."

Finney came to realize that "the reason their prayers were not answered was because they did not comply with the revealed condition upon which God had promised to answer prayer. They did not pray in faith in the sense of expecting God to give them the things they asked for."

Finney learned the power of believing prayer, and, as a result, saw mighty miracles and thousands of salvations. Revival had come to America again.

Finney believed prayer was the number one ingredient for revival and for changing the hearts of men and women. He told of one woman "in feeble health" in Oneida County, New York, who in the fall of 1825, "kept praying more and more" until there was a breakthrough in her spirit. She proclaimed, "God has come!" A revival broke out throughout that region and many were saved.

As soon as he would arrive in a town, Finney would look for people who were committed to prayer. He knew that there could be no breakthroughs without earnestly calling on the Lord.

When he arrived in Antwerp, New York, few people even had an interest in the things of God. As he sought out praying people, only "two or three women in humble circumstances were mentioned." But Finney knew this was all he needed. They started praying and revival descended.

These revivals spread throughout America, and it was reported that a thousand congregations "have been visited within six months...with revivals of religion."

When Frenchman Alexis de Tocqueville visited America in 1831 and 1832, he quickly recognized the importance of religion for the American people. "The religious aspect of the country was the first thing that struck my attention." He saw that the Christian faith was foundational for every part of life, and how it provided the glue that kept America together.[54]

Yes, God had visited America. Its citizens were not perfect, but America was, indeed, a Christian nation.

Chapter Eight

REVIVALS IN THE CITY AND COUNTRY

AS AMERICA HAS CHANGED AS A COUNTRY, GOD HAS responded in ways as diverse as our people and our natural resources.

The great westward migration provided major spiritual challenges. This was a move unprecedented in history. None of our Pilgrim Fathers could have dreamed how expansive the West would prove to be. And no one could imagine the riches – and dangers – that awaited the pioneers as they settled in the prairies and mountains.

But Americans continued to take risks. Rumors and rewards kept attracting people from the East, as well as other nations, who flocked to fill our expanding boundaries.

Who settled these lands? Some were families. Others were fortune-seekers, adventurers, or people just wanting a fresh start. While some were Godly, many were crude, immoral, and irreverent, and so the West became known as a wild, turbulent, uncertain place.

But God had not forgotten America, and He continued to touch lives through camp meetings.[55]

On the American frontier, there were no elaborate buildings, but as God moved, people gathered from miles around. Camp meetings were held just about anywhere and at any time. People came together in places like "the banks of a wooded stream where there was ample shade, water, and pasture." If necessary, trees were cleared and seats were built.

The conditions often were harsh but that didn't stop anyone. Men and women were hungry for God!

Many of those who came to camp meetings lived in tents of their own, but others stayed in covered wagons which might be "pitched in a circle around the place of meeting." Sometimes the services went on all day, even into the night, when temperatures often were brutally cold and the meeting place had to be lit with lanterns and campfires.

The camp meetings might continue for weeks. Whole communities were known to abandon everything except the most necessary work. Why? Because God was moving. His Spirit fell on those who were hungry for His Presence, and their lives were changed.

As people were drawn together to seek God, amazing things happened. In these often hostile conditions, God's Spirit was present in powerful ways. People would be convicted of their sins and asked forgiveness. Thousands were saved, and tens of thousands of lives were transformed. America was changed.

But revivals weren't confined to the frontier.

"THE EVENT OF THE CENTURY"

One of the most powerful and important spiritual outpourings in American history began in New York City. It started with a prayer meeting held on September 23, 1857, by Jeremiah Lanphier.

At the time, the city was filled with despair and plagued by financial problems, bank failures, and widespread unemployment. Even though he was only a businessman, Lanphier had accepted the challenge of his church to conduct a visitation program.

He invited people to join him in prayer, distributing a handbill that called on men to leave the business world for a moment and spend time focusing on eternity and God. He challenged others to join him in a time of dedicated prayer.

Only six men attended the first meeting, but more joined every week. And "within six months, 10,000 businessmen were gathering daily" for prayer. Soon, meeting rooms filled and churches throughout the city opened their doors to accommodate the crowds. Before long, even police and fire stations were being used for prayer.

These meetings generated front page stories in newspapers, and prayer meetings began springing up throughout America and the world. As a result, more than a million people were saved! Salvations came at a staggering rate. For two years, at least 10,000 people each week were giving their hearts to the Lord, and some weeks this number reached 50,000.

This revival was no respecter of denominations. People in every walk of life and theology were changed by the power of God. The Lord moved in such a miraculous way that in some New England towns "it was hard to find a person who was unconverted." A traveling businessman told a meeting in Boston that he had come from Omaha, Nebraska. "On my journey east, I have found a continuous prayer meeting... about two thousand miles in extent."

Perry Miller, a historian from Harvard University, called this revival "the event of the century,"[56] even more important than the War of 1812, the Civil War, inventions like the telephone, or the settling of the West!

This was known as a "quiet" revival. Finney himself commented that "Inquirers needed more opportunity to think than they had [in the previous awakening] when there was so much noise." Finney also observed that this was largely a revival of laypeople, without any dominant pastors or preachers.

"I WILL BE THAT MAN"

One of the many people whose life was impacted by this revival was a shoe salesman who had moved to Chicago. After one of his merchants told him about a prayer meeting, the salesman decided to attend for himself. His life, and America, would never be the same.

The man was Dwight L. Moody, and in June 1860, he dedicated himself full-time to the Gospel. His ministry eventually extended worldwide as he held revival meetings throughout the United States and Europe.

What made Moody different? R.A. Torrey said he felt that "the first thing" was that "he was a fully surrendered man." Moody was "imperfect," but "he was a man who belonged wholly to God." Early in his ministry, Henry Varley told him, "It remains to be seen what God will do with a man who gives himself up wholly to Him." Moody reportedly replied, "I will be that man."

Moody told him one day, "Torrey, if I believed that God wanted me to jump out of that window, I would jump." That is the degree to which he committed His life to God.

As many as one million people became Christians under Moody's ministry. One of the secrets of his effectiveness was a commitment to prayer.

Torrey once commented, "Time and time again, he was confronted by obstacles that seemed insurmountable, but he always knew the way to surmount and to overcome all difficulties...He knew and believed in the deepest depths of his soul that 'nothing was too hard for the Lord' and that prayer could do anything that God could do."

On many nights, Moody and Torrey would pray "far into the night...crying to God, just because Mr. Moody urged us to wait upon God until we received His blessing. How many men and women I have known whose lives and characters have been transformed by those nights of prayer and who have wrought mighty things in many lands because of those nights of prayer!"[57]

GOD'S HELP IN TROUBLED TIMES

In many ways, the revival of 1857-1859 helped prepare the nation for the Civil War. But while the country was torn by that horrible conflict, God did many other miraculous works.

Early in the war, sin appeared to sweep through both armies. Camps were filled with vices including gambling and profanity. One Confederate soldier reportedly said that "if the South is overthrown, the epitaph should be 'died of whiskey.'" But God began to move, and in the Fall of 1863, what has been called the "Great Revival" began in both the northern and southern armies.

According to J. William Jones, a chaplain in the Confederate army, about 10% of the soldiers in the Army of northern Virginia accepted Christ. Night after night troops participated in prayer meetings, worshiped God, and heard the Gospel proclaimed. Camps frequently were filled with the sounds of Gospel songs. Confederate Chaplain William Bennett reported "that fully one-third of all the soldiers in the field were praying men and members of some branch of the Christian Church."

But revival was felt in the North as well. In the Army of the Potomac, chapels became so full that "many men were frequently turned away." It has been estimated that perhaps as many as 100,000 Confederate and 200,000 Union troops accepted Christ during the Civil War.[58]

After the conflict ended, these soldiers brought their renewed faith back to their churches and homes. Many became pastors, evangelists, and missionaries who impacted the nation and the world for the Gospel.

Leaders both in the North and South turned to God and openly drew their strength from Him. Abraham Lincoln found himself facing situations for which he had no clear answers. He sought God for wisdom and peace, direction and discernment. He increasingly leaned on his faith to sustain and guide him.

> **Lincoln sought God for wisdom and peace, direction and discernment. He increasingly leaned on his faith to sustain and guide him.**

After Lincoln was assassinated in 1865, a document he had written in September 1862 entitled "A Meditation on the Divine Will" was discovered among his papers. This document showed how Lincoln realized that ours was a nation whose only hope was in God. He struggled to grasp His purposes.

"The will of God prevails," Lincoln wrote. "In great contests each party claims to act in accordance with the will of God." Yet he felt that "in the present civil war it is quite possible that God's purpose is something different from the purpose of either party; and yet the human instrumentalities, working just as they do, are of the best adaptation to affect his purpose."[59]

In the years following the Civil War, a new wave of immigrants came to America. Like those Pilgrims who arrived on our shores in the 17th century, many journeyed here for religious reasons. The expansion of America in the West was fueled by thousands of these God-fearing men and women.

Many were overwhelmed with the freedom they found to worship God. G. D. Hall was one of those who ministered to these grateful immigrants. In August 1899, Hall held a series of services in a small prairie town where he "found a hunger after God's Word so intense seldom found elsewhere. They had a great appetite for the Gospel."

Countless lived in sod houses and "endured many severe trials." But Hall found that their faith "has given them power to soar above it." Many of the people were "poor but they are happy in Jesus and satisfied with their lot."[60]

In the process, these men and women helped form a "Bible Belt" made up of people for whom Christianity was something they lived every day. They depended on God for the rain to grow crops, for protection against storms and danger, for the health of their families and livestock, and for every meal.

Church life and their faith were the foundation for their lives.

INSPIRATION FROM WALES

As God moved by His Spirit throughout America, He also brought a powerful revival to Wales that shook the world. On the surface, Wales at the end of the 19th century was a dark and hopeless place, filled with sin. It may remind us of America today.

Many Welsh Christians feared their country was lost. One leader wrote that "nothing short of an outpouring of the Spirit from on high will uproot" the tares from the church "and save our land from becoming a prey to atheism and ungodliness."[61]

Christians realized that only God could change this condition, and many began praying with increased fervor. They became burdened for the Lost and longed for a move of the Holy Spirit.

God began answering their prayers and stirred the heart of a young man named Evan Roberts. In the spring of 1904, Roberts was praying one night when he felt "taken up to a great expanse" into a time of "communion with God." Then, for three months, he was awakened every night a little after one o'clock, spending four hours with the Lord.

One morning, as he joined other students in prayer, one phrase burned in his heart: "Lord, bend us." The words lingered, and when they gathered again for prayer, the power of the Holy Spirit became so compelling that he fell to his knees in tears.

As Roberts pleaded with God to bend him to His will, he felt God give him a deep "compassion for those who must bend at the judgment." He "felt ablaze with a desire to go through the length and breadth of Wales to tell of the Savior."

After that encounter, he traveled throughout Wales, preaching in church services, calling on people to turn to God. Revivals started springing up.

A newspaper account described how revival came to Loughor, a village in southwest Wales, through Roberts' ministry. Meetings were held "every night attended by dense crowds," beginning at 7:00 p.m. and lasting until past 3:00 a.m. Many who had never attended church before were "making public confession of their conversion." It was said that everyone was talking about revival.

As the Spirit descended, "people dropped down from their seats as if they had been struck" and starting "crying for pardon."

The fires of revival quickly spread and others became caught up in the move to seek God. Joseph Jenkins was one Welsh man who pleaded for the anointing of the Holy Spirit upon his life. God granted new boldness and power. People yearned for God, turned from sin, were saved, and filled with the Spirit. A visitor to one of Jenkins' meetings commented, "I have never seen the power of the Holy Spirit so powerfully manifested among the people as at this place just now."

As God moved by His Spirit throughout America, He also brought a powerful revival to Wales that shook the world.

The revival brought significant changes in the lives of the people. After revival fell on the city of Treorky, "feuds and personal animosities" were put aside. Hearts overflowed with love for each other. The newspaper spoke of the "improved conduct in the mines." The workers had become "better workmen." There was a "lessening of drunkenness" and people in the coal mines talked "about religious matters" and prayed "together in their work places."[62]

AZUSA STREET

This revival not only changed Wales but also influenced America. In December 1904, Frank Bartleman and his family moved to Pasadena, California.[63] They had no income and were forced to live by faith. But he believed that God had called him there. Yet, within two weeks, their youngest child, Esther, died.

Although filled with grief, he felt compelled to start preaching. He stated, "I could only live while in God's service. I longed to know Him in a more real way and to see the work of God go forth in power. A great burden and cry came in my heart for a mighty revival."

Bartleman realized that the Lord was "preparing me for a fresh service."

He began to preach at a local mission and said, "I was greatly burdened for souls." He continued to preach in services throughout the area nearly every day, but also spent time passing out tracts and witnessing in bars and to prostitutes.

Soon God began to move. Revival swept through Southern California. Men and women felt an urgency to pray. They saw that the world was filled with sin and wickedness. In a spirit of prayer and humility, Bartleman recalled, "We were shut up to God in prayer in the meetings, our minds on Him." He wrote how "the Spirit dealt so deeply" with those who were gathered, and "people were so hungry" for God.

This was not just casual prayer, but fervent and deep. "It was held sacred, a kind of 'holy ground.' Men sought to become quiet from the activities of their own too active mind and spirit, to escape from the world for the time, and get alone with God...Men would spend hours in silence there, searching their own hearts in privacy, and securing the mind of the Lord for future action."

Bartleman joined others who sought God, and revival came to Pasadena. But they were not content and began to "pray for an outpouring of the Spirit for Los Angeles and the whole of Southern California." They prayed with intensity. This dedication to prayer and intercession eventually led to the great revival at Azusa Street.

This outpouring of the Spirit of God swept the nation. Thousands were converted. New churches formed. Lives were changed, and there was an outgrowth of missions and evangelism.

GOD'S SOVEREIGN PURPOSES

Wales experienced the power of the Spirit, and so did Azusa Street. God kept moving throughout America and the world. In the years that followed, there were revivals under the ministry of men like Billy Sunday. During the 20th century, God's Holy Spirit was manifested through great evangelistic crusades and television ministries. In recent years, we also have seen revivals in places like Toronto, Brownsville, and Pensacola.

Only our Heavenly Father knows why revival visited these places and not others. But these moves of God teach us many things and provide examples for us to follow.

They remind us God can do anything. He can change hearts and lives. Even the most cold and hardened sinner can be shaken by His power. He can transform whole countries and entire cultures.

Over and over again, God has sent revival when His people seek Him in fervent, concentrated, committed, and even "violent" prayer. When they repent of their sins. When they seek to live in righteousness and holiness. When they lay aside their personal interests and become committed wholeheartedly to His Kingdom and His righteousness.

Today, America and the world need a mighty outpouring of the Holy Spirit of God.

We as a people need to return to the Lord. We need to seek His face and cry out for a Divine visitation of His presence, power, and glory to sweep across our nation and the world. We need to plead with the Almighty, asking, "Lord, visit us in our time. Forgive our sins. Our only hope is in You! We hunger to know You and, by Your power, to live righteous and holy lives. Use us."

This is my prayer. Will you make it yours too?

Chapter Nine

TIMES OF CRISIS

IN A MOMENT OF GREAT IRONY, THE BARNA GROUP released a study on September 10, 2001, reporting that 74% of the adults in America said they were "concerned about the moral condition of the nation."

When asked the basis on which they form their moral choices, 44% cited their desire to do whatever will bring them the most pleasing or satisfying results. Only 24% said that they "lean primarily upon religious principles and teaching or Bible content when making moral decisions."[64]

The day *after* this study was released, America was shaken to its core with terrorist attacks. Suddenly, in this hour of crisis, many Americans had a different perspective. By the millions, they cried out to God. Churches were filled. There were public services. Even commercial TV networks preempted their schedules for religious observances. Leaders of all parties prayed for America.

Immediately after the attack, attendance at worship services increased 25%. The percentage of Americans who said religion was very important to them rose from 57% before the attacks to 64% afterward. People prayed, with 74% in September 2001 saying they would pray more.[65]

While this surge of interest in faith gave many people the comfort and assurance they needed during this time of crisis, sadly, there was little lasting change.

Within weeks, attendance at worship services reverted to pre-attack levels. The percentage of Americans who believed in an "all-powerful, all-knowing God" dropped from 72% before the attacks to 68% afterward. And confidence in absolute moral truths dropped from 38% to 22%.

The more time passed following the tragedy, the less people seemed to know what to believe. In December 2001, 45% of Americans were attending religious services almost once a week or more. But by May 2002 that percentage dipped to 42%, the same level it was in June 2001.

In a study conducted by American Demographics, people in this nation were not living up to their own promises. In October 2001, 18% of Americans said they planned to attend religious services more regularly after Sept. 11. However, "just 8% of them actually were doing so a few months later." Bible reading and prayer increased for a short time, but then diminished to pre-attack levels.

Many people had taken for granted that America would never be attacked and assumed our country had a "special protection from God." But by March 2002, only 48% told the Pew Forum they agreed with this statement. Most Americans simply weren't sure any more.

Another surprising development is that in the post 9-11 world, fewer people said the Bible was the "source of the principles or standards on which they base their moral and ethical decisions." This had shrunk to only 13%.

What were people counting on? Twice as many people (25%) said they depended on their feelings, while 14%

depended on "the lessons and values they remember from their parents."

It's frightening to learn that millions of Americans trust so strongly in their feelings. But this helps explain why America has drifted so far from the Truth and why so many people are deceived and confused.

THE LORD SAVED "SQUANTO"

Just as we cried out to God on September 11, 2001, Americans have turned to Him in times of crisis in the past. In response, He has been gracious to us and answered our prayers.

When the Pilgrims landed in 1620, they desperately needed help to survive the harsh winter. They were experiencing hunger and sickness, and it wasn't clear if they would survive.

Then one day, a Native American unexpectedly walked into the settlement. The Pilgrims did not know what to expect, and they were stunned when the man spoke to them in clear English. He said, "Welcome!" This seemed like the most unlikely of miracles.

The man's name was Samoset, but the Pilgrims called him "Squanto."

Years earlier, Squanto had been taken to England by a fisherman who had visited the New England area. He lived there for nine years, where he not only learned the Queen's English but also heard the Gospel and became a Believer.

When John Smith made a voyage to America in 1613, Squanto was brought along as an interpreter and was rewarded with his freedom. But in 1614, "he and nineteen others from his tribe were kidnapped by another Englishman and sold into slavery in Malaga, Spain. There he worked as a house servant before managing to escape to England. In 1619, he joined an English expedition headed for the New England coast."

When he returned to his home in America, he discovered his tribe had been destroyed by a plague, making him the last surviving member of the Pawtuxet tribe. Had he not been taken, he, too, would have died from the plague that destroyed his village. But God spared Squanto and equipped him to help the Pilgrims by teaching them how to "plant corn, catch fish, trap beaver, and prepare summer fruits for the winter. He also served as an interpreter and diplomat in their dealings with other Indian tribes."[66]

In fact, his presence likely saved the Pilgrims from death. They had cried out to God for help, and He miraculously answered their prayers.

PROCLAMATIONS OF PRAYER

Throughout our history, Americans have continued to cry out to Him during times of crisis.

In May 1797, the country faced a possible war with France. How did President John Adams respond? By calling the nation to a day of fasting and prayer. Many in the press mocked him for this decision, but the American people knew the nation needed God in this hour of peril. Adams later recalled with satisfaction how the churches were filled with praying people and how God answered their prayers, sparing America from the crisis.[67]

When the British attacked America in 1812, many felt the situation was hopeless. But President James Madison proclaimed two national days of prayer. He had not forgotten what God had done 15 years earlier. Following a successful moment in the war, he proclaimed a "National Day of Public Humiliation, Fasting & Prayer to Almighty God." And after the war ended, Madison declared a "National Day of Thanksgiving & Devout Acknowledgment to Almighty God."[68]

Then as America faced the fear and uncertainty of a Civil War 50 years later, Abraham Lincoln increasingly turned to the Almighty. He urged Americans to do the same. On March 30, 1863, he called for a "National Day of Humiliation, Fasting and Prayer." He knew God was sovereign over the affairs of men and nations, and that He had a righteous standard. Lincoln wrote, "It is the duty of nations...to own their dependence upon the overruling power of God, to confess their sins...with assured hope that genuine repentance will lead to mercy."

> The American people knew the nation needed God in this hour of peril . . . . the churches were filled with praying people and God answered their prayers, sparing America from the crisis.

As Americans fought and died, Lincoln looked to God for help and perspective: "The awful calamity of civil war...may be but a punishment inflicted upon us for our presumptuous sins."

Lincoln knew America had been blessed by God and that He held our country to higher standards: "We have been the recipients of the choicest bounties of Heaven....We have grown in numbers, wealth and power as no other nation has ever grown. But we have forgotten God. We have forgotten the gracious Hand which preserved us in peace, and multiplied and enriched and strengthened us; and we have vainly imagined, in the deceitfulness of our hearts, that all these blessings were produced by some superior wisdom and virtue of our own."[69]

A HERITAGE OF FAITH

On the evening of D-Day, June 6, 1944, while American troops were fighting to establish beach heads on the coast of Normandy in France, President Franklin Delano Roosevelt led the nation in his "D-Day Prayer." He asked his fellow countrymen to join him in praying:

> *Almighty God: Our sons, pride of our nation, this day have set upon a mighty endeavor, a struggle to preserve our Republic, our religion, and our civilization, and to set free a suffering humanity. Lead them straight and true; give strength to their arms, stoutness to their hearts, steadfastness in their faith. They will need Thy blessings... O Lord, give us faith. Give us faith in Thee; faith in our sons; faith in each other; faith in our united crusade. Let not the keenness of our spirit ever be dulled...With Thy blessing, we shall prevail over the unholy forces of our enemy...Thy will be done, Almighty God. Amen.*[70]

When Roosevelt died suddenly the next year on April 16, 1945, Harry S. Truman became President. In his first address to Congress, Truman said,

> *At this moment I have in my heart a prayer. As I have assumed my duties, I humbly pray Almighty God, in the words of King Solomon: 'Give therefore Thy servant an understanding heart to judge Thy people, that I may discern between good and bad: for who is able to judge this Thy so great a people?' I ask only to be a good and faithful servant of my Lord and my people.*[71]

Many others also have led America in prayer at crucial

turning points: Presidents of all parties, congressmen and senators, governors and mayors.

These men and women knew that prayer, belief in God, and a commitment to Christianity were part of our heritage as a nation. And they shared these convictions themselves.

While this calling reflects our religious heritage and the Godly traditions that remain strong in our country, there is another sobering aspect to our pleas for God to save us.

God knows our hearts.

As He did with the Israelites who repeatedly turned away from Him in rebellion, the day may come when He will no longer respond to our cries for rescue. We must depend on God *daily,* not only in times of crisis. He is looking for people who will commit their very lives to Him. People who will serve and obey Him. People who will faithfully keep His commandments. People who will live righteous lives.

America had put God
first, and because we
acknowledged God as
the Source and Giver
of life, we found favor
in His sight.

Chapter Ten

A NATION FOUNDED ON LIBERTY

AMERICA IS A "MELTING POT." WE ARE A NATION OF immigrants, and the sons and daughters of immigrants. Our history is unique and so are our citizens. Who are we, this diverse people who call ourselves Americans?

* We are the Puritans who fled England and came here to worship God and evangelize a new world.

* We are the Huguenots who fled France.

* We are the Scotch, Irish, and Catholics who sought religious freedom and a home for our people.

* We are the Jews who fled Czarist Russia and Hitler's Nazi Germany.

* We are the slaves who were brought here against our will, most often in inhumane and brutal conditions.

* We are the Irish who sailed to our shores during the potato famines of the 19th century.

* We are the Italians who came to America after the Great Panic of 1872.

* We are the Scandinavians who arrived to farm the land and worship God.

* We are the Chinese who came to work the railroads and find hope.

* We are the Vietnamese boat people, the lucky ones who didn't perish in the China Sea.

* We are the Cuban refugees who crammed into tiny boats to cross the Caribbean to escape tyranny.

* We are the Latin Americans pouring across our southern borders in hopes of a better life.

Together, we form the United States of America. And together, we have built the greatest nation on earth. And how did it happen?

Not because we were wise or strong. Or because we had great leaders. Or because of our natural resources or geographic location. Or because of our educational institutions or free enterprise system. It happened because so many in America had a personal relationship with Jesus Christ. He was the Lord of their lives. *Their* will was to do *His* will. They loved God and His Word. He was a real and vital part of their daily lives.

Because America had put God first and we were a people who sought to serve Him, and because we acknowledged God as the Source and Giver of life, we found favor in His sight.

That's why God has a special destiny for America. That's why God's hand was on our nation, why God blessed us as a people, and why He protected us, time after time after time.

* Our country was built by pioneers willing to risk their lives to form a nation where God was honored and the Bible was taught.

* We have persevered through oppression and endured times of darkness, trusting God to help and guide us.

* Even when we made mistakes and did the wrong thing, God was merciful to us.

* We have experienced wave after wave of revivals that renewed our commitment to God, and swept away sin and everything polluting our personal and national life.

TO BE FREE!

Since it was presented to America by the French government in 1884, the Statue of Liberty has symbolized the spirit of America. This majestic monument, located in New York Harbor, carries a plaque bearing these words: "Give me your tired, your poor, your huddled masses yearning to breathe free." Why have people come here? To be free!

Since the time our forefathers came to Jamestown and Plymouth, our nation has been a beacon for people throughout the world who desire liberty. But this freedom has always been based on a belief in the God of the Bible and a commitment to His Word.

The Bible says, *"Where the spirit of the Lord is there is liberty"* (2 Corinthians 3:17). It is the Spirit of God that is the key to our freedom, and it has been because of America's liberty that we have been able to gain wealth and power. Because of God's blessings, America has become a powerful, wealthy country. By some estimates, we consume 92% of the world's resources...and we must never forget the history of how it came to greatness.

When this nation was founded, many doubted it would survive. They could not imagine a true democracy was even possible. But by the grace of God, we have more than survived.

In fact, the U.S. is the oldest democracy in the world. Some speak of the democracies in the antiquities, such as the government of ancient Greece. But the Greeks didn't really have a democracy. About half of their population was comprised of slaves, while half of those who were supposedly "free" were women; however, they couldn't vote or own property. In fact, women weren't even counted in a census.[72] So did ancient Greece have a democracy? Well, yes, if you were a man who was lucky enough to be part of the remaining 25%!

> The more we look across the globe, the greater the realization that our freedom here in the United States is a rare gift from God.

But there has never been anything quite like America. Let's compare a few of the other notable nations on this earth to our nation...

China is the largest country in the world, with a population of almost 1.5 billion people and the longest continuous history of any nation. When God looks down from Heaven, He sees mostly Chinese! Yet in all the 3,500-year-history of these people, they have never experienced the freedom you and I have in America.

India is the world's second largest nation on earth, with more than one billion people. What a magnificent past India's people share. Yet, in all their history through thousands of years, they've enjoyed only about 50 years of democracy as we know it.

We could talk about the young and frail democratic experiments in the former Soviet Union, Indonesia, or Brazil. We could speak of dictatorships and struggling democracies in South and Central America and Africa. But the more we look across the globe, the greater the realization that our freedom here in the United States is a rare gift from God. So I ask you, my fellow Americans, my fellow Christians, what will we do with this treasured and rare blessing of life, liberty, and the pursuit of happiness?

Throughout our existence, we have been blessed by the truth that where the Spirit of the Lord is, truly there *is* liberty (2 Corinthians 3:17). And where there is liberty, there will be free enterprise and commerce, confidence and wealth. And *there* God pronounces His blessing.

But there is another side to God's favor. He expects us to take responsibility for what we've been given. We have an obligation to faithfully serve Him and accomplish His purposes. A responsibility to honor Him, keep His commandments, and place Him first in our lives.

WHAT HAPPENED TO AMERICA?

When you closely examine American history, it's impossible *not* to see the hand of God at work in the birth, development, and building of this nation. It's impossible *not* to see how God has protected us. And it's impossible *not* to conclude that America was founded by Christians.

Yes, no matter what a few revisionist judges, atheists, professors, writers, politicians, and media pundits might claim, America was founded by men and women of Christian faith who came to these shores for religious freedom, who arrived here with a missionary spirit to bring the Light of the Gospel to native Americans and to make a difference in the new world for Christ.

Yet, it's equally true that America has not always been faithful to God. At times, we've been a nation on fire for Him. But there also have been much longer periods when we've been lukewarm, or even cold, toward Him. There have been times when we have turned our backs on God, perhaps more now than ever before.

Over and over again God has shown us that if we will return to Him, He will bring revival to our land and our people. The words of 2 Chronicles 7:14 could not be more relevant for America than today:

> If my people, which are called by my name, shall humble themselves, and pray, and seek my face, and turn from their wicked ways; then will I hear from heaven, and will forgive their sin, and will heal their land.

Yet within our lifetime, we've seen a decline in commitment to Christianity. Gallup reports that in the 1970s and 1980s, as many as 40% of Americans believed that the Bible was the "actual word of God." But today that percentage is only 28%. Almost 20% believe it's an "ancient book of fables," while almost half say the Bible is inspired, but "not everything in it should be taken literally." In other words, they think they can choose what they want to believe and ignore (or reinterpret) the rest![73]

No wonder there is so much confusion in our country! Is there any question that we need to return to God? To return to the Bible? To return to righteousness?

Our culture has been confused by ridiculous movies and books that have claimed belief in God is a delusion. That Jesus was married and had children. That there are "alternative" Gospels that were repressed...and much more. These all are the imaginations of desperate people, misled by their own mistaken minds (and fed from the pit of hell!).

Our basic beliefs and heritage have been eroded to the point that we are facing a post-Christian society. Why? What has happened to America?

One reason we have arrived at such a place of desperate need is because we haven't faithfully committed to our children the things we were taught and believed in. Generations have slipped further away from His Truth and reality in their lives. There is widespread ignorance of Scripture. Many churches do not even teach the Word of God. In fact, some teach that the Bible is not God's Word at all.

It seems we have a generation of preachers in American pulpits who have chosen "ministry" as a vocation or job instead of being chosen by the Lord with a spiritual calling from Almighty God. They want to expound their own values and beliefs instead of teaching their congregations what the Bible says.

We have a generation of preachers whose own personal values and beliefs don't mirror the Word of God. Jesus spoke of these when He said, *"This people honors Me with their lips, but their heart is far from Me. In vain they worship Me, teaching as doctrines the precepts of men"* (Matthew 15:8-9). If this is the example of many so called "shepherds," how can we expect the "sheep" to be any different?

APPALLING IGNORANCE

Today, Biblical ignorance has reached epidemic proportions. For example, a recent study revealed that 60% of Americans "can't name five of the Ten Commandments." And "50% of high school seniors think Sodom and Gomorrah were married."[74]

Because so many do not know God's Word, they are ignorant of His standards. They have allowed the world to corrupt their understanding of Truth, and they have accepted compromise.

A recent study revealed that fewer young adults are willing to base their views of morality on Biblical Truth. Instead they "bend moral and sexual rules to their liking." Rather than being concerned with the Bible's moral absolutes, many Christians are adapting their lives to the standards of the world.

Shockingly, only three out of 10 of these young adults "embraced the concept of absolute truth." Less than half of them feel we "should determine what is right and wrong morally by examining God's principles." What do they believe? Nearly half said that "ethics and morals are based on 'what is right for the person.'"

What is even more disturbing is that Christians have almost the same views as non-Christians! Either they don't know what the Bible says or they've chosen not to believe it![75]

Just consider these facts about today's "born again" Christians:

* 80% agree with the statement, "The Bible teaches that God helps those who help themselves" (even though this is not in the Bible).

* 49% agree that "the devil, or Satan, is not a living being but is a symbol of evil" (ignoring what the Bible says concerning Satan).

* 39% maintain that "if a person is generally good, or does enough good things for others during their life, they will earn a place in heaven" (ignoring that the Bible says we are not saved by our works but through our faith and by confessing Jesus Christ as our Savior and Lord).

* 30% claim that "Jesus Christ was a great teacher, but He did not come back to physical life after He was crucified" (disregarding witnesses' testimony recorded in the New Testament and in other works of history from that time).

* 29% contend that "when He lived on earth, Jesus Christ was human and committed sins, like other people" [76] (despite the fact that Scripture teaches He was sinless).

And remember that these are people who say they are "born again"!

The vast majority of Americans profess to believe in "God," but who...or what...do they really mean? There are countless definitions and many interpretations.

A recent Harris Interactive poll suggested that 42% of U.S. adults are not "absolutely certain" there is a God. Only 29% said they believe God "controls what happens on Earth." And 44% said they believe that God "observes but does not control what happens on Earth."[77]

> Rather than being concerned with the Bible's moral absolutes, many Christians are adapting their lives to the standards of the world.

Think about this fact: A majority of American adults (51%) believe that Christians and Jews, and Muslims all worship the same God! In particular, young people believe that those who follow a Judaic-Christian belief system and those who follow Islam both have the same God. But this is *not* what the Bible says.

As the children of Israel were preparing to enter the Promised Land, Moses told them, *"Their rock is not our Rock"* (Deuteronomy 32:31). He knew they would be among people with many different gods and religions, and that some would say that "they all are the same." But he wanted Israel to know there is only one God, and He is not the Allah of Islam or the "feel good" god of nature. He is the God of Abraham, Isaac, and Jacob!

Our young people are the most vulnerable to these ideas: 61% of young adults say they were "churched at one point during their teen years but they are now spiritually disengaged." They become inactive and independent as adults, stop attending church, and stop reading the Bible.

At the same time, a growing number are willing to change their religious experience. Fifteen percent have changed from one religious preference to another. And 10% say they have moved away from religion altogether.[78]

THE DANGERS OF RELATIVISM

We've strayed far from the days of our Founding Fathers, when everyone knew the Bible, and it was the basis of our laws and daily life. Nowadays, many Americans don't think it's possible to determine what is "decent." They reject the concept of one "Truth." Contrary to what the Bible teaches, they feel there are many paths to God and that they are all acceptable.

We live in a global community and regularly interact with those from different cultures. Through immigration, people from a wide variety of religions have come into the U.S. However, while more Americans seem determined to define "religion" in their own terms, the majority sense something is wrong. While we're not necessarily willing to make changes to improve morals, Gallup reports that as of 2006, 77% of Americans hold negative views about the nation's moral climate, and 81% say things are getting worse. These numbers are much higher than in the past.[79]

But we shouldn't be surprised by these results. We've chosen to ignore God's Word. We've eliminated Him from our schools. We've filled our minds with TV programs, films, and other media containing content that encourages immorality and pokes fun at God and Christian beliefs. We've filled many of our church pulpits with pastors who don't even believe in the Bible.

Today we have choices to make. Will we follow the world in believing there are many options? Or will we believe, as Peter told the Jewish leaders in the book of Acts, that there is salvation in no one else besides Jesus (Acts 4:12)? Will we believe Jesus Himself, who says, *"I am the Way, the Truth, and the Life"* (John 14:6)?

While our culture seems to have no problem making fun of Christians, many Believers feel it's wrong to "offend others" by standing for Biblical Truth and righteousness. Instead we respond to the pressure to say nothing and let people believe whatever they want to believe. We're encouraged to be "politically correct" and not to take a stand for fear we might hurt someone's feelings.

How ridiculous! Can we imagine Isaiah worrying about being politically correct? How about Jeremiah or Ezekiel? Or John the Baptist? Or Jesus Himself?

Yet millions of Christians are spiritually crippled because they've been brainwashed to think like the world, ignoring the fact that many use political correctness to ridicule and repress Christianity.

One reason why many people argue there is no such thing as "Truth" is because our culture is filled with the teaching of "relativism." Relativism is "any philosophical position which maintains that there are truths and values, but denies that they are absolute."[80]

"ENOUGH!"

In his powerful book, *Hell? Yes!* Robert Jeffress describes what happened to him when he stood up for Biblical principles and spoke out against relativism.[81]

Jeffress learned that the library in his home town of Wichita Falls, Texas, had added two books to its collection: *Daddy's Roommate* and *Heather Has Two Mommies*. Both books tell the story of children being raised by homosexual couples.

Outraged, he referred to these books in a sermon based on what happened to Sodom and Gomorrah. Standing on the Word of God, he concluded, "No society can afford to condone what God has condemned." It was now a "time when Christians need to take a stand against evil...It's time for God's people to say, 'Enough!'"

> You cannot be a follower of Jesus and believe that all "beliefs are equal, and all truth is relative." This is not an option.

Pastor Jeffress simply was fulfilling his responsibility as a preacher of the Gospel, doing nothing different than God's people have done since the time of Noah. He was following in the tradition of prophets like Isaiah and Jeremiah, Amos and John the Baptist, and other men of God in our history like Jonathan Edwards.

Little did he know he had ignited a firestorm. Word of his sermon spread across the nation. Stories were carried by newspapers like *The New York Times*, wire services, and national television and radio programs. The town was split. Jeffress said, "The editor of the local newspaper wrote an editorial condemning me for promoting censorship and suggesting that I should be jailed for my act of civil disobedience."

But what shocked Jeffress the most was the criticism he received from Christians. "One prominent minister of a large denominational church in our community stood in his pulpit one Sunday during the furor and said *he* was 'not called upon to judge, but to tell others about love.'" A letter to the editor criticized him for spreading "hatred and intolerance."[82]

This is how many people today believe. They have concluded that no "one way" is right. Facing a world filled with conflicting religions with each claiming to be "right," many even have abandoned the concept of "Truth." In fact, many people have become obsessed – not with Truth but with "tolerance." It sounds like such a wonderful concept, doesn't it? Perhaps it even sounds like a Christian duty and responsibility.

Some confuse tolerance with unconditional love. But they are not the same. While the Bible teaches us to love everyone, it also teaches there is right way and a wrong way to live. There is only *one Truth, one Life, one Way to the Father:* Jesus (John 14:6).

But tolerance preaches there is no *one* way. Thomas Helmbock, executive vice president of the national Lambda Chi Alpha fraternity, recently wrote, "The definition of new...tolerance is that every individual's beliefs, values, lifestyle, and perception of truth claims are equal...There is no hierarchy of truth. Your beliefs and my beliefs are equal, and all truth is relative."[83]

But to accept this definition is to reject the Bible. You cannot be a follower of Jesus and believe that all "beliefs are equal, and all truth is relative." This is not an option.

Jesus said, *"Enter through the narrow gate; for the gate is wide and the way is broad that leads to destruction, and there are many who enter through it. For the gate is small and the way is narrow that leads to life, and there are few who find it"* (Matthew 7:13-14). Not every way leads to salvation. There is only one way.

THE NARROW ROAD

To many, this broad road sounds wonderful, warm, compassionate, understanding, nonjudgmental, and logical. Why not? It allows us to do anything we want and not worry about the consequence of our actions. But to believe this is to deny the Bible and reject the very tenets of the Christian faith. This broad road leads to destruction, and this is where we are headed as a nation unless we start seeking the *"narrow gate"* (Matthew 7:14).

We need to realize that when we take stands for Truth and for the Gospel, we will face criticism. We may be accused of trying to be morally superior and arrogant, rigid, or out-of-touch. We may hear comments like those famed talk show host, Phil Donahue, made to Dr. Michael Brown: "You can't stand there righteously and tell me you know what's good for me…You can't tell me that there's only one way for me to get to heaven. Nobody is that smart."[84]

Such an attitude is becoming the norm in America today. A belief that rejects absolute Truth. A belief that rejects the Bible. A belief that rejects the Christian faith. A belief that everything is relative. A belief that we just need to be "tolerant."

People like Donahue fail to see that rejecting Truth means opening up our society to hell. Why have we seen such an increase in wickedness and immorality? Because people are being taught that there is no Truth. If everything is relative, then there is no right or wrong.

Today, it is considered "normal" to treat all religions as

equal...except that all too often, Christians are persecuted and restricted, while other religions are given encouragement and public support. Suddenly, it's okay to be a Muslim or Buddhist, but not a Christian. And Muslims and Buddhists can express their views freely, while Christians are repressed.

In Dearborn Heights, Michigan, the Muslim call to prayer by a cleric or imam can be heard five times daily over loud speakers throughout the community. Try having a Christian pastor lead people in prayer once a day, let alone five times a day, over a public address system covering entire communities, and see what people have to say!

REAPING WHAT WE'VE SOWN

Many were shocked by the brutal massacres of 33 students at Virginia Tech University in April 2007. Our society has been outraged by murders, racism, discrimination, gang warfare, and other forms of violence. Yet they fail to see how we have brought this on ourselves.

By denying the concept of Truth, we have rejected God. By saying everything is relative, we're saying that everything is OK. For some, this is all the justification they need to commit murder and rape, rob and steal, cheat and lie, defy God's Laws and mock Jesus and His followers.

By tolerating violence, immorality, and godlessness on our television programs, films, music, books, and video games, we've created a culture where some people feel violent crime is a viable option and anything is acceptable.

In a report issued after the Virginia Tech massacres, the Barna Group reminded us of the facts, pointing out that parents have sat by while the media has continued to flood our culture with violence and ungodliness. We continue to reap what we've sown:[85]

* By the time an American child is 23 years old, as was the killer in Virginia, he will have seen countless murders among the more than 30,000 acts of violence, to which he is exposed through television, movies and video games.

* By the age of 23, the average American will have viewed thousands of hours of pornographic images, which diminish the dignity and value of human life.

* After nearly a quarter century on earth, the typical American will have listened to hundreds of hours of music fostering anger, hatred, disrespect for authority, selfishness, and radical independence.

* The typical worldview of a person in their early twenties promotes self-centeredness, the right to happiness and fulfillment, the importance of personal expression in all forms, the necessity of tolerating aberrant or immoral points of views, allows for disrespect of other people and the use of profanity, and advances forms of generic spirituality that dismiss the validity of the Judeo-Christian faith.

* The average adolescent spends more than 40 hours each week digesting media, and the typical teenager in America absorbs almost 60 hours of media content each week. For better or worse, the messages received from the media represent a series of unfiltered, unchaperoned worldview lessons.

How many massacres will it take before Americans wake up to the harmful impact of violence and immorality in the media? What will it take for parents to take more seriously their responsibility before the Lord to raise their children in a Godly way?

When will our country realize the horrible consequences of removing the Bible from our children's education and instead filling their minds with Satan-inspired images designed to deprive them of God's blessings while teaching them a lifestyle filled with sin? When will we stop pretending that everything is "relevant" and realize there is only one Truth? One Way? One Life?

Yet we continue to see and hear this philosophy of relativism and "tolerance" expressed every day. It's taught in the schools, and it also characterizes the lifestyle of celebrities and rock stars, who ignore Biblical principles and do whatever they please...and these are the very ones so many of our children are idolizing and imitating!

The end result is everywhere, underlying the philosophy of many TV programs and films. It is the justification for countless decisions made by people of all ages. We hear "experts," and even friends, encourage us to do or believe whatever we want.

We've become like Israel in the time of the judges: *"In those days there was no king in Israel; every man did what was right in his own eyes"* (Judges 17:6). That was a time of crime, violence, and godlessness. But we, too, live in an era where people are doing what is right in their own eyes, and we all are suffering the consequences.

But for the Christian, the only important question is this: What does *God* have to say? What does *His Word* say? This is where we must look if we truly want to understand true righteousness.

God's Word teaches us
there are consequences
for our actions,
and the choices we
make determine these
consequences.

Chapter Eleven

GOD'S STANDARDS AND EXPECTATIONS

THE BIBLE TELLS US THAT *"RIGHTEOUSNESS EXALTS a nation, but sin is a disgrace to any people"* (Proverbs 14:34). This truth has been proven throughout the annals of time. Yet countless leaders and nations have chosen to believe they are different, that they don't have to be concerned with God's Word. They have sought short-term pleasures, power, and wealth, and have been willing to forget righteousness. But eventually, they all will learn that the only kind of praise and reward which matter are those that originate from God.

Tragically, they will discover that sin and a life of sin lead only to *"disgrace."*

God's Word teaches us there are consequences for our actions, and the choices we make determine these consequences. The principles that are true for individuals are also true for nations:

* Just as people reap what they sow, so do nations (Galatians 6:7).

* The same way individuals have been given resources and "talents" and are judged based on how they invest them (Matthew 25:14-30), these same principles apply to nations. We learn a great deal about governments by what they do with their human and natural resources.

* We know the heart of people by what comes out of their mouths and what is expressed in their lives (Matthew 15:19). Nations also reveal what is important to them by their actions and rhetoric.

* Individuals are stewards of what they have been given by God, and as such, are expected to be good servants (Luke 12:42-43). This same principle applies to nations.

* In the sight of God, each person is honored for being a faithful servant and a good steward, and for obeying His Word and being obedient to His call on their lives (Luke 19:17, Matthew 24:45-46). This also is the pattern for nations. They are exalted by the decisions they make and what they do with their God-given resources.

And so the whole world is observing how we as a nation conduct ourselves, make decisions, and use our resources.

In his first letter to the Corinthians, Paul provided a perspective on what we must learn from history and the Bible:

For I do not want you to be unaware, brethren, that our fathers were all under the cloud and all passed through the sea; and all were baptized into Moses in the cloud and in the sea; and all ate the same spiritual food; and all drank the same spiritual drink, for they were drinking from a spiritual rock which followed them; and the rock was Christ.

Nevertheless, with most of them God was not well-pleased; for they were laid low in the wilderness. Now these things happened as examples for us, so that we would not crave evil things as they also craved. Do not be idolaters, as some of them were; as it is written, 'THE PEOPLE SAT DOWN TO EAT AND DRINK, AND STOOD UP TO PLAY.'

Nor let us act immorally, as some of them did, and twenty-three thousand fell in one day. Nor let us try the Lord, as some of them did, and were destroyed by the serpents. Nor grumble, as some of them did, and were destroyed by the destroyer. Now these things happened to them as an example, and they were written for our instruction, upon whom the ends of the ages have come (1 Corinthians 10:1-11).

These are truths that apply to us as individuals *and* to our country.

A PERMANENT IMPRESSION

Philosopher George Santayana is known for his observation that "those who cannot remember the past are condemned to repeat it." The Bible – and even the pages of history – are filled with warnings and lessons God has given us. These are *"examples for us"* that were *"written for our instruction"* (1 Corinthian 10:6). We must learn from the past…or we will be doomed to repeat what has happened before, over and over again.

The specific Greek words Paul chose when writing his letter to the Believers at Corinth clearly communicated to them that God intended for the Israelites' history to "leave a deep mark or impression" on those who would follow in their footsteps, as if "struck by a blow" or as an "object molded into a firm shape." Their experiences were to serve as a "stamp made by a die" that repeats an image every time because it is so clear, solid, and distinguishable.

Why did God include these examples in Scripture, these deep impressions? To help us not crave the wrong things and make the same mistakes. To help us realize the consequences of our actions before it's too late. To help us change while there is still time.

In order to learn our lessons and realize how serious God is about the situations we face, we just need to look to the Bible and learn from the many examples He has given us.

> God included examples in Scripture . . . . to help us realize the consequences of our actions before it's too late.

Countless people today believe that "man is the center of the universe." In this worldview, there are no concerns for the Almighty. In fact, many films, books, TV programs, and other products have praised people for standing up to the notion of religion and even fighting against God.

In his celebrated anti-Christian manifesto, philosopher Friedrich Nietzsche wrote that he believed in trying and questioning everything. He said, "'This is my way; where is yours?' Thus I answered those who asked me 'the way.' For *the* way – that does not exist."[86]

Untold millions believe this false truth, claiming that all of us are "free moral agents," able to do whatever we want, insisting that no one particular way is "*the* way."

Many authors, celebrities, scientists, and educators have celebrated the "heroic" battle to become free of Christian influences. They have listened to the "wisdom" of philosophers like Bertrand Russell who professed, "I do not think that life in general has any purpose. It just happened." He argued "Outside human desires there is no moral standard."[87]

They have listened to thinkers such as Jean-Paul Sartre who wrote, "God is dead. Let us not understand by this that he does not exist or even that he no longer exists." Sarte believed "man can will nothing unless he has first understood that he must count on no one but himself; that he is alone, abandoned on earth...with no other destiny than the one he forges for himself on this earth."[88]

What a hopeless worldview! Yet millions of people blindly accept this attitude toward life and reject the possibility of life with God.

FOR OUR GOOD

The Bible gives us a completely different perspective. In fact, like all of life, it begins with God: *"In the beginning God created the heavens and the earth"* (Genesis 1:1). From the dawn of creation, we see His creative design and His miraculous hand at work.

In His interaction with the first human beings, God made it clear that His intention was to bless Adam and Eve and do everything for their greatest good. He also gave them free will and the opportunity to make choices.[89] But there were restrictions and rules, and there were consequences to their choices. They needed to decide for themselves if His words really were true, and if He would do what He said He would do.

When Satan came to Adam and Eve, he did not just

"tempt" them. He caused them to doubt God. To disbelieve His Word. To be confused and believe his lies (Genesis 3:4-6).

The *truth* was that they could eat freely from *"every tree of the garden"* except the tree of the knowledge of good and evil. If they obeyed Him, He would protect them and provide everything they needed. But God also promised consequences if they disobeyed: *"In the day that you eat of it you shall surely die"* (Genesis 2:16-17).

However, the serpent – Satan – deceived Eve, telling her that God was withholding blessings and not telling them the truth: *"God knows that in the day you eat of it your eyes will be opened, and you will be like God, knowing good and evil"* (Genesis 3:4-5). Eve was attracted by this explanation, so she chose to disobey God. Adam joined her, and sin entered the world.

The first man and woman learned many things from their choice. First, they discovered Satan is a liar. He promised them freedom and pleasure but instead, they were forced to leave the garden God lovingly had prepared for them. They spent the rest of their lives in hard toil and experience the pain of death, a grief God never intended for them to suffer.

But they also were awakened to the fact that God's Word is true, and that He is holy and had created the world with eternal standards. They learned some things are right, while others are wrong, and that there are consequences for their actions.

A MAN WHO WALKED WITH GOD

The people of Noah's time discovered God is not kidding about His standards and His judgment. Some behavior is acceptable to Him, while some behavior is not. He is kind and patient, yet there is a limit to His patience, and judgment is necessary for those who violate His principles.

In Noah's day, God saw a world filled with wickedness and that every intent of the thoughts of people were *"only evil continually."* But Noah was different. Why? Because he *"was a righteous man, blameless in his time; Noah walked with God"* (Genesis 6:5-9).What made him righteous? He walked with God and obeyed Him.

While judgment fell on the rest of mankind, Noah and his family were spared. And he discovered that God looks out for and protects those who serve Him and keep His ways.

FOUR REASONS FOR JUDGMENT

It's important for us to understand the impact that any wickedness has on God. The Bible tells us He is perfectly holy, pure, and righteous (Psalm 145:17; Revelation 15:4). He cannot abide the presence of any form of sin.

So sin, evil, or wickedness separates us from God. We cannot have fellowship with Him as long as sin is in our lives. Sin leads to His displeasure and to the removal of His blessing. And if the wickedness is as rampant as it was in the time of Noah, it can lead to His punishment.

Why did God send judgment to the people of Noah's day? There are four reasons that will give us insights into the crisis America faces today.

1. People were doing things that were wicked. There was not just *some* level of sinfulness once in a while. This wickedness was *"great"* (verse 5). There was so much iniquity that God could no longer tolerate it.

When God created the world, He saw that it was *"good"* (Genesis 1), and He never wanted His creation to embrace evil. But that's what people were choosing to do.

2. More than merely doing what was sinful, the people on earth had evil hearts. They never stopped thinking about things that were wrong and wicked. God's judgment was that *"every intent of the thoughts of men's hearts was only evil continually"* (verse 5).

Their concepts were evil and so were their purposes. Just like a potter takes the clay and molds an object, so people were forming the deeds of their lives from the evil and wickedness residing in their hearts.

3. The earth was corrupt. People had spoiled the world that was *"good"* when God created it. They had perverted what had been pure and ruined what had been faultless. More than just seeing that the world was filled with wickedness, God saw how *"all flesh had corrupted their way on the earth."*

The Creator was not merely upset with those who infected the innocent and polluted the pure. He was displeased because this kind of depravity had become a pattern for the way people lived.

Their lives were filled with corruption, including their habits, manners, and course of life. Their moral character was corrupted, spoiled, and polluted with sin. And *"their way"* that was defiled was like a road, and they had strayed off course. In fact, the whole earth was headed in the wrong direction.

4. The earth was filled with violence. It was everywhere. The crime rate must have been terrible, with people stealing, killing, cheating, and hurting others. While all this was true, the original Hebrew used in this passage conveys even more. It suggests moral violence. They were acting, thinking, and speaking in ways that violated God's holiness, and they were seeking unjust gain.

If the behavior of humanity so grieved God *then* that it caused Him to destroy His creation, we can trust the same things must offend Him *today*. And our disobedience will cause Him to take action!

We should be alarmed when we look at our present circumstances. We, too, are living in a world filled with wickedness, corruption, and violence. Will God be forced to judge us, as He did the people of Noah's time? Unless we change and repent, and return to righteousness, judgment seems inevitable. There *is* hope for America…but the choice is ours!

The Almighty had given His guarantee, but there was an "if," a condition: Abraham *had* to do *his* part.

Chapter Twelve

THE MERCY AND JUDGMENT OF GOD

TO GRASP THE IMPORTANCE OF RIGHTEOUSNESS, WE need to understand that God is a God of Covenants. Noah was the first person to learn this truth. God told him, even before he entered the ark: *"I will establish My covenant with you"* (Genesis 6:18).

The Lord revealed much more on this subject to Abraham, telling him, *"I will establish My covenant between Me and you."* As part of this Covenant, He gave Abraham a promise: *"I will multiply you exceedingly"* (Genesis 17:2).

Abraham learned that God never changed and that His Word was always true. Once the Lord had made a Covenant with him, it was guaranteed to be fulfilled. It was His promise, His commitment. Abraham discovered he could count on God in every situation. He always meant exactly what He said, and He fulfilled every word He spoke.

But Abraham also learned that God's agreements are *conditional.* The Almighty had given His guarantee, but there was an "if," a condition: Abraham *had* to do *his* part. If he wanted to receive what God had promised, he had to obey Him and do what He required.

The conditional nature of God's Covenants tells us why righteousness is so significant. Abraham had to trust God every step of the way and believe He would keep His promises. The Bible says he *"believed the Lord, and He credited it to him as righteousness"* (Genesis 15:6). But he also had to obey.

Abraham had choices to make. Because he knew God's Covenants were conditional, *he* had to decide what *he* was going to do. If he did *his* part, God would do *His*. But if Abraham disobeyed and went his own way, God was under no obligation to fulfill His promises. And as Abraham believed and obeyed, the Lord fulfilled His Covenant with him.

SODOM AND GOMORRAH

As Abraham began applying these truths in his own life, he also learned what happens to people who violate God's principles. Who do not obey Him. Who do not live in righteousness.

Like Noah, he saw that God could not condone sin and that His standards could not change. He also saw that as people made choices throughout their lives, they were determining the kind of results they would receive. Blessings or curses. And even judgment.

Abraham became a firsthand witness of the Creator's righteous actions with the judgment of Sodom and Gomorrah. These cities were not interested in righteousness or morality. They had made a decision to be "tolerant." They had an "anything goes" philosophy. In fact, their standards remind us of America today.

Here was a culture that not only tolerated homosexuals and their lifestyle; it actually *encouraged* all forms of promiscuity. There was no moral code and no concern for God's Truth or righteousness. Life was not held in sanctity; instead, people did what they wanted without restraint.

The men and women of these cities were so wicked that God decided He had no choice but to bring judgment.

Lot, Abraham's nephew, had settled in Sodom because it was an area that was pleasing to his eyes and *"well watered everywhere"* (Genesis 13:10). Little did Lot know that he had decided to live in a place where sin was so widespread, it was destined to be condemned by God.

This is in part why America has arrived at the sad place where we are today. Christians haven't been tormented by the sin around us.

The Bible tells us Lot was *"oppressed by the sensual conduct of unprincipled men."* He is described as a righteous man living among the unrighteous. But even more, the Bible says his righteous soul was tormented day after day with their lawless deeds (2 Peter 2:6-8).

When was the last time you personally felt pain and anguish by the actions of unrighteous people around you? This is in part why America has arrived at the sad place where we are today. Christians haven't been tormented by the sin around us. We have looked the other way, not wanting to "offend" and unwilling to confront sin. Worse than that, we have not personally fallen on our faces before God and asked Him to forgive our sins and heal our land.

God's judgment of Sodom and Gomorrah shows us clearly that He is holy. That His standards are eternal. And that we suffer the consequences whenever we violate His rules.

God condemned the cities of Sodom and Gomorrah to destruction by reducing them to ashes, having made them an *example* to those who would live ungodly *thereafter*, yet He rescued righteous Lot who was distressed by the evil conduct of unprincipled men. Peter went on to state that these unscrupulous men *"suffered wrong as the wages* [earnings, consequences, and rewards of their actions] *of doing wrong"* (verse 13).

So first we read that God condemned the cities of Sodom and Gomorrah. Second, we learn He reduced them to ashes. Why? Because of the immorality of the people. The Bible records God's response to unrighteousness:

> *For this reason God gave them over to degrading passions; for their women exchanged the natural function for that which is unnatural, and in the same way also the men abandoned the natural function of the woman and burned in their desire toward one another, men with men committing indecent acts and receiving in their own persons the due penalty of their error.*

> *And just as they did not see fit to acknowledge God any longer, God gave them over to a depraved mind, to do those things which are not proper, being filled with all unrighteousness, wickedness, greed, evil; full of envy, murder, strife, deceit, malice; they are gossips, slanderers, haters of God, insolent, arrogant, boastful, inventors of evil, disobedient to parents, without understanding, untrustworthy, unloving, unmerciful;*

> *and although they know the ordinance of God, that those who practice such things are worthy of death, they not only do the same, but also give hearty approval to those who practice them* (Romans 1:26-32).

Third, God said He was making these cities an example to generations and nations that were to come of what the penalty and consequences would be for living similar lifestyles.

Finally, God cautioned that the unprincipled men who behaved in this fashion would suffer as the wages of their wrong doing.

A DIVINE WARNING

God describes the consequences of immorality when He says that your flesh and body will be consumed (Proverbs 5:11). In Proverbs 7:23, God warns that an *"arrow will pierce through your liver"* and it will cost you your life. Imagine that, a medical diagnosis written thousands of years ago of the consequences of sexual immorality. Who could have known then that one of the primary organs in the body targeted by AIDS would be the liver? Who could have known that this would lead to death? Only the Creator. And God gave His warning.

In spite of God being so clear that immoral behavior will cost a person their life, people persist in their belief that they can do whatever they please without consequences.

Almost everywhere we turn today we can see the onslaught of the gay and lesbian agenda as they press to make acceptable what they call an "alternative lifestyle" and what the Bible calls an abomination (Leviticus 18:22). God says He destroyed Sodom and Gomorrah, not just because of their immorality, but as examples to those who would live ungodly thereafter.

What more of an example or warning do we need? Unprincipled men and women today want to call those of us who stand up for Biblical morality "homophobes." They try to silence any claim that their behavior is deviant, sinful, or abnormal.

The subject of sin in our society is very unpopular. It's not politically correct to talk about iniquity or the wages of sin.

The Bible says, *"There is none righteous, not even one"* (Romans 3:10). Scripture also tells us that every one of us have sinned and fallen short of the glory of God (Romans 3:23). Christians aren't perfect people, they are just forgiven and have been made the righteousness of God in Christ Jesus (2 Corinthians 5:21).

People outside of Christ and the Church too often want to claim that the Bible is a hate book. They state that Christians despise people who live contrary to the teachings of God's Word. This isn't true. The Bible doesn't teach Christians to harbor hatred for anyone. However, let's be clear: Scripture repeatedly teaches us to hate sin and evil (Psalm 97:10; Proverbs 8:13; Amos 5:15).

When will we as the Body of Christ stand up and say, "Enough is enough!"?

There's a big difference between hating the sin versus hating the sinner. We are to despise the sin while loving the sinner. This is why the Bible says that while we were yet sinners (all of us), God demonstrated His own love toward us, by sending His only Son Christ to die for us (Romans 5:8).

It's not enough that homosexuals want to be free to live their chosen lifestyle of sin; no, they want us to teach our children in public schools that there's more than one way for couples to live in relationship with each other. They want to distort and pollute the Bible and society's definition of marriage. They want to redefine the parameters and definitions of marriage beyond one man and one woman to include men with men and women with women. What's next? The legalization of pedophilia or bestiality?

When will we as the Body of Christ stand up and say, "Enough is enough!"?

In the example of Sodom and Gomorrah, we see God's judgment *and* His mercy. He allowed Lot and his family to be saved. But we also see how He gives us opportunities to choose.

And we reap the consequences of our actions.

A HOLY NATION

Moses learned firsthand about God's holiness when he saw a bush on fire but not being consumed by the flames. God told him, *"Do not come near here; remove your sandals from your feet, for the place on which you are standing is holy ground"* (Exodus 3:1-5).

Moses and the children of Israel learned that God had standards, and He kept His Covenants. He remembered His promises, and He sent Moses to rescue His people from bondage in Egypt.

After God miraculously delivered them from the Egyptians, they declared, *"Who is like You among the gods, O LORD? Who is like You, majestic in holiness, awesome in praises, working wonders?"* (Exodus 15:11) They realized He was holy.

God told the Israelites they were special people and that they were to live lives pleasing to Him. They were to *"be to Me a kingdom of priests and a holy nation"* (Exodus 19:6).

Whenever they came into the presence of anything ungodly, they were to eliminate it without compromise. When God delivered their adversaries into their hands, He commanded them to *"utterly destroy them. You shall make no covenant with them and show no favor to them"* (Deuteronomy 7:2). For ungodliness there could be no tolerance!

If the Israelites were to be His people and receive His blessings, they had to learn to...

...utterly destroy all the places where the nations whom you shall dispossess serve their gods, on the high mountains and on the hills and under every green tree. You shall tear down their altars and smash their sacred pillars and burn their Asherim with fire, and you shall cut down the engraved images of their gods and obliterate their name from that place (Deuteronomy 12:1-5).

He warned them they would be surrounded by people who would tempt them to abandon their faith in God and lure them to follow their sinful ways.

When the LORD your God cuts off before you the nations which you are going in to dispossess, and you dispossess them and dwell in their land, beware that you are not ensnared to follow them, after they are destroyed before you, and that you do not inquire after their gods, saying, "How do these nations serve their gods, that I also may do likewise?" (Deuteronomy 12:29-30).

Sadly, the children of Israel failed to heed this warning. They allowed themselves to be tempted and lured away. And they suffered the consequences.

To understand the crisis America is facing today, we must read the Bible, learn from the examples God has given us there, and heed His warnings. They are as true for us today as they were for the Israelites in Bible times. We must choose to stand for righteousness, or we, too, will experience the consequences of our choices.

Chapter Thirteen

THE LAW AND RIGHTEOUSNESS

IN THIS BOOK I'VE FREQUENTLY REFERRED TO "righteousness" and being "righteous." We hear and use these words often, but maybe it's not clear to you what they mean.

What exactly *is* "righteousness"? And what does it mean to *be* "righteous"?

Simply, these terms mean to live according to God's standard. To put His Word into practice in our lives. To obey Him through the things we say and do.

Both of these words come from a root word that means "straightness." God has provided us with the "straight" and right way to life. We are "righteous" when our lives line up with His changeless standards.

We cannot live righteous lives without His Word and without knowing His Divine rules for living. Then when we know them, we need to apply them daily.

By definition, God *is* righteous. And He gave His people the Law so they would know how to live and what to do to achieve success, receive His protection and blessing, and to stay out of trouble. He gave the Law for their good:

> *O Israel, you should listen and be careful to do it, that it may be well with you and that you may multiply greatly,*

just as the LORD, the God of your fathers, has promised you, in a land flowing with milk and honey (Deuteronomy 6:3).

But the Israelites had to learn that if they disobeyed God's Law, there were consequences. They could expect to fall away and be corrupted *if* they lived among people who did not serve Him. The Law was to guide them and set their standards:

These are the statutes and the judgments which you shall carefully observe in the land which the LORD, the God of your fathers, has given you to possess as long as you live on the earth (Deuteronomy 12:1).

He wanted the best for them and said, *"Oh that they had such a heart in them, that they would fear Me and keep all my commandments always"* (Deuteronomy 5:29). In these words we feel His compassion and concern. He wanted them to succeed, to enjoy His blessings continually. Yet He knew they would not always have *"such a heart in them."* They would not always fear Him or keep His commandments. And as a result, they tragically would experience His judgment.

OBEDIENCE THROUGH FAITH

The children of Israel told God they would fear Him and keep all His Divine laws. But He knew they would not always be obedient and faithful...that they would be tempted to follow the ways of the people around them...that they would drift away, forget their promises, and fail to keep His commandments.

What was His solution? To remind them of the Law He had given them: *"So you shall observe to do just as the LORD your God has commanded you; you shall not turn aside to the right or to the left"* (Deuteronomy 5:32). It was through practical obedience and faithfulness in their daily lives that they would be able to stay true and faithful.

But to know what to do, the Israelites first needed to know and understand His Word, which provided them with the knowledge necessary to continue enjoying His blessings, to stay clear of problems and temptations, and to keep from falling: *"You shall walk in all the way which the LORD your God has commanded you, that you may live and that it may be well with you, and that you may prolong your days in the land which you will possess"* (Deuteronomy 5:28-33).

We cannot be righteous in God's sight on our own merits. The Bible tells us that we become righteous through *faith*.

While God focused on their obedience, He also warned that none can be righteous on our own. The Almighty cautioned, *"Do not say in your heart when the LORD your God has driven them out before you, 'Because of my righteousness the LORD has brought me in to possess this land,' but it is because of the wickedness of these nations that the LORD is dispossessing them before you"* (Deuteronomy 9:4).

As the prophet Isaiah said, *"We are all like an unclean thing, and all our righteousness are like filthy rags; we all fade as a leaf, and our iniquities, like the wind, have taken us away"* (Isaiah 64:6). We cannot be righteous in God's sight on our own merits.

Ultimately, this is why Jesus came to die for us. He came to take away our sins and make us righteous in God's sight. How?

The Bible tells us that we become righteous through *faith*. As Paul wrote, his desire was to be found in Christ, *"not having a righteousness of my own derived from the Law, but that which is through faith in Christ, the righteousness which comes from God on the basis of faith"* (Philippians 3:9).

"DO" THE LAW

Scripture explains that because of Jesus, we are given legal standing before God as righteous people. Even though each of us is a sinner, based on Jesus' death for our sins, God accepts us, forgives us, and pronounces us as righteous.

Paul tells us that, in Christ, God now acts in our lives to make this possible. We are given a *"new self, created to be like God in true righteousness and holiness"* (Ephesians 4:24).

Being New Testament Christians, we are no longer under the Law. And we are warned against depending on our own righteousness. But nothing changes the importance of living according to God's Word. The Bible still provides the standards by which we are to live. Scripture tells us...

Prove yourselves doers of the word, and not merely hearers who delude themselves. For if anyone is a hearer of the word and not a doer, he is like a man who looks at his natural face in a mirror; for once he has looked at himself and gone away, he has immediately forgotten what kind of person he was.

But one who looks intently at the perfect law, the law of liberty, and abides by it, not having become a forgetful hearer but an effectual doer, this man will be blessed in what he does (James 1:22-25).

Jesus said we show our love for Him through our obedience (John 14:15).

RIGHTEOUS THROUGH THE WORD

While many Christians are quick to talk about "grace" and

God's love, they are reluctant to speak of the importance of obedience and righteousness.

Many people have the same attitude toward their lives. It can be easy for them to justify their actions, but they seem hesitant to open their minds and hearts to the penetrating, convicting work of the Holy Spirit. They don't want to *"look intently at the perfect law,"* which is God's Word.

James said that such people deceive themselves. They may think they are pleasing God, but they aren't putting His Word into practice, and they are blind to the true state of their hearts.

God does not want this to happen. He wants us to realize that His Word is perfect. But we must read and study the Bible and then determine to put its Truth into practice. Then we can ask Him to examine our thoughts and deeds in light of His pure Word and set us free.

We cannot pretend that we will ever be perfect, *"for all have sinned and fall short of the glory of God,"* and we only are *"justified as a gift by His grace through the redemption which is in Christ Jesus"* (Romans 3:23-24).

God has made a way for us to be forgiven:

> *"If we say that we have no sin, we are deceiving our-selves and the truth is not in us. If we confess our sins, He is faithful and righteous to forgive us our sins and to cleanse us from all unrighteousness. If we say that we have not sinned, we make Him a liar and His word is not in us"* (1 John 1:8-10).

Is righteousness important to God? Absolutely.

Is His Word still necessary? It certainly is.

We can't be righteous without God *and* His precious Word.

Our Founding Fathers
recognized that America
needed to be based on
a belief in God and
founded on His Word.

Chapter Fourteen

AMERICA AND THE LAW

THE LAW HAS BEEN IMPORTANT TO AMERICA EVER since the Pilgrims signed the Mayflower Compact and established the principle that this was to be a country based on law. Our Forefathers realized the necessity of jurisprudence, and they based our laws on the Bible and a belief in the God of Scripture.

At the time of the writing of our Constitution, the most influential legal authority in the English-speaking world was Sir William Blackstone. Born in 1723, Blackstone achieved significant influence as a barrister, but his greatest impact was his four-volume *Commentaries on the Laws of England,* which he wrote between 1765 and 1769, just before our War for Independence.

In the words of the Encyclopedia Britannica, these were "the best known description of the doctrines of English law." This was a work that "became the basis of university legal education in England and North America." It remains possibly the most influential work on law ever written in the English language.

These volumes became required reading for every lawyer in America at the time, including Thomas Jefferson and James Madison. His opinions were cited in countless court cases and were considered not just authoritative but also definitive.

Blackstone believed that all law had its source in God. He wrote that when God created matter, He "established certain rules." He did the same when He created man:

> Considering the creator only a being of infinite power... and of infinite wisdom, he has laid down only such laws as were founded in those relations of justice, that existed in the nature of things antecedent to any positive precept.

> These are the eternal, immutable laws of good and evil, to which the creator himself and all his dispensations conforms...the law of nature, being coequal with mankind and dictated by God himself, is of course superior in obligation to any other. It is binding over all the globe and all countries, and all times: no human laws are of any validity if contrary to this.[90]

Along with Blackstone, our Founding Fathers recognized that America needed to be a nation of laws, and they were to be based on a belief in God and founded on His Word. That is why they worked so hard to create a Constitution that would stand the test of time. Thomas Jefferson once said, "We are not a world ungoverned by the laws and the power of a superior agent. Our efforts are in his hand, and directed by it; and he will give them their effect in his own time."[91]

American courts and judges continued to be based on principles such as the ones Blackstone argued. In fact, a Supreme Court ruling in 1811 stated, "Whoever strikes at the root of Christianity tends manifestly to the dissolution of civil government."[92]

These principles were still in place a hundred years later. In 1892, David J. Brewer, Associate Justice of the Supreme Court, summarized a view that was commonly held throughout the judicial system. He wrote, "Christianity has been so wrought into the history of this republic, so identified with its growth and prosperity, has been and is so dear to the hearts of the great body of our citizens that it ought not to be spoken of contemptuously or treated with ridicule."[93]

He reviewed our history and confirmed what the facts show: "Christianity was a primary cause of the first settlement on our shores." Our forefathers clearly recognized that Christianity was "a controlling factor in the life of the people."

In fact, Christianity "was in terms declared the established religion, while in several the furthering of Christianity was stated to be one of the purposes of the government." Through Brewer's review of the history of our country, he showed that "the calling of this republic a Christian nation is not a mere pretense but a recognition of an historical, legal, and social truth."[94]

But slowly, during the 20th century, things began to change. Judges began to redefine our legal history. They started forgetting about the foundation that Blackstone and our Founding Fathers took for granted.

One of the most significant and tragic results has been the creation of the myth of the "separation of church and state."

THE "SEPARATION" MYTH

If you took a poll, most people would probably say they believe that the Constitution guarantees a separation between church and state. Even many Christians believe this. But this is not true! In fact, this subject has been totally misrepresented. Liberals have shouted about this "separation" for so long and so loudly that many people believe it's true. But the reality is that our forefathers *never* intended for us to have separation of church and state!

Somehow, many people today, including the media, politicians, and judges, base their views on religion in America on this concept. But saying this phrase over and over again doesn't make it true. Neither does shouting it louder and louder. The amazing fact is that this phrase never appears in the Constitution. And it doesn't even occur in any documents from the period when the Constitution was written. In addition, it doesn't occur in any legal papers written by anyone who signed the Constitution. So from where did this false idea originate?

The first comments appear to have been made in the early 17th century by Roger Williams, founder of Rhode Island. But the most often quoted reference is a letter Thomas Jefferson wrote to a group of Baptist pastors in Danbury, Connecticut, in 1802. He wrote:

> *Believing with you that religion is a matter which lies solely between man and his God, that he owes account to none other for faith or his worship, that the legislative powers of government reach actions only, and not opinions, I contemplate with sovereign reverence that act of the whole American people which declared that their legislature should make no law respecting an establishment of religion, or prohibiting the free exercise thereof, thus building a wall of separation between church and state.*[95]

It is upon this one letter that the entire concept of the "separation between church and state" is based.

Yet those who cite this document have serious flaws in their logic. The context in which Jefferson wrote to this group of Baptist pastors must be taken into consideration. Context is critical.

You've no doubt heard the silly example of taking things out of context when it comes to Scripture itself. Take for example two verses taken totally out of context: *"And Judas went away and hanged himself"* (Matthew 27:5) and *"Go ye and do likewise"* (Luke 10:37 KJV). It's ridiculous to say that the Bible is teaching us to go and hang ourselves based on quoting two verses of Scripture completely removed from their framework. The same is true with Jefferson's letter.

What was the context of Jefferson's letter? The fact is, a group of Baptist pastors had written to him, concerned that the United States would adopt a state religion. Their fears were that by adopting a state religion similar to what had happened in Great Britain with the Church of England, Americans would find themselves without religious freedom and liberty. Jefferson was writing them to allay their fears that no such state religion would be established as provided for in the Constitution. "...legislature would make no law respecting the establishment of religion, or prohibiting the free exercise thereof..."

The "wall of separation" Jefferson spoke of was in the context of a State-established religion. He simply was saying to them, "No way. It's not going to happen. Don't worry about it."

Keep in mind that Jefferson, the author of the Declaration of Independence, was also our third President. However, he was not directly involved in the writing of our Constitution. Even if he had been, and even if someone were to take his letter out of context or interpret it contrary to this explanation, his letter to these Baptist pastors merely represented his personal opinion in 1802 and as such, has no legal standing.

Like all the Founding Fathers, Jefferson was concerned about preventing the establishment of a state church. There is no indication he or anyone else at the time could have imagined this "wall" being formed to restrict our Christian faith.

Yet the courts have done that very thing. One of the most pivotal moments in the creation of this myth took place in

1947 when Justice Hugo Black delivered the opinion of the Supreme Court in the case, *Everson v. Board of Education of the Township of Ewing Et. Al.*

This case involved a New Jersey law that authorized local school boards to pay the costs of transporting students to and from private schools, including Catholic schools. A local resident, Arch R. Everson, filed a lawsuit claiming this action aided religion. He contended this violated the New Jersey State Constitution and the First Amendment of the U.S. Constitution.

Everson lost the lower court ruling, but appealed to the U.S. Supreme Court. This provided Judge Black with the opportunity to make a landmark ruling regarding what he felt was the proper relationship between Church and State.

As part of the justification for his decision, Black quoted Jefferson's letter of 1802. In fact, the only foundation for his argument was that one letter. No laws had been passed, and there was nothing about this subject in the Constitution.

In recent years, case after case has been decided with arguments built – not on the Constitution or the intentions of the Founding Fathers – but on that one letter.

THE "ROCK" OF THE REPUBLIC

If anti-Christian forces can quote this letter, *we* should be able to quote statements from noted historic leaders of our nation such as...

* **John Quincy Adams:** "The highest glory of the American Revolution was this, it connected in one dissolvable bond, the principles of civil government with the principles of Christianity."

* **Andrew Jackson:** "The Bible is the rock on which our republic rests."

* **Woodrow Wilson:** "America was born a Christian nation. America was born to exemplify that devotion to the elements of righteousness which are derived from the revelations of the Holy Scriptures."

* **Calvin Coolidge:** "The foundations of our society and our government rest so much on the Teachings of the Bible that it would be difficult to support them if faith in these teachings would cease to be practically universal in this country."

* **Harry Truman:** "The fundamental basis of this nation's laws was given to Moses on the Mount. The fundamental basis of our Bill of Rights comes from the teaching...If we don't have the proper fundamental moral background, we will finally wind up with a totalitarian government which does not believe in rights for anybody except the state." [96]

* **The U.S. Supreme Court** itself, which, in the 1892 case, *Church of the Holy Trinity v. United States*, ruled, "Our laws and our institutions must necessarily be based upon and embody the teachings of the Redeemer of mankind...Our civilization and our institutions are emphatically Christian...This is a religious people. This is historically true. From the discovery of this continent to the present hour, there is a single voice making this affirmation...we find everywhere a clear recognition of the same....This is a Christian nation."

We should be able to talk about the prayers that have been prayed in Congress, in the White House, on television and radio, in speeches, books, and letters, and by Presidents, congressmen, senators, and judges.

From a spiritual perspective, we need to realize there is a deeper issue involved here: the remaking of America by imposing on our country another philosophy without God, and even eliminating Christianity from the mainstream of American life.

We've also seen a major change in recent years. Today, many judges have decided to become more "active" in interpreting the laws and interjecting their personal opinions regarding what they think the laws mean or should mean. In the process, they are *reinterpreting* what our Founding Fathers meant and intended, and have used their position of power to assert their own philosophy about life, religion, and government.

UNHOLY RULINGS

To see the impact of this judicial philosophy, just take a sober look at the rulings of our courts and the laws that have been considered in recent years:

* Court rulings which say that the words "one nation under God" in our Pledge of Allegiance violate the First Amendment

* Laws that allow homosexual lifestyle, behavior, and "marriages"

* School systems which mandate the teaching that homosexuality is just as "normal" as heterosexuality

* Laws that allow schools to openly distribute condoms to kids

* Laws that restrict the right to conduct Bible studies or witnessing on "public" or government property

* Cities that shut down Christmas displays on public or government property

We've even seen judges rule that it's illegal for a kindergarten teacher to recite a simple poem that express gratitude to God:

We thank you for the flowers so sweet;
We thank you for the food we eat;
We thank you for the birds that sing;
We thank you God for everything.

While our Founding Fathers, and even our courts, encouraged everyone to read the Bible, in recent times we've seen the Supreme Court issue rulings that warn *against* reading the Scriptures:

> *If the posted copies of the Ten Commandments are to have any effect at all, it would be to induce the schoolchildren to read, meditate upon, perhaps to venerate and obey, the Commandments...This...is not a permissible state objective under the Establishment Clause [First Amendment].*[97]

Is there any wonder that America faces God's judgment? Is there any doubt that we, as a people, need to repent? Can there be any question that we need to return to righteousness?

How do the American people feel about these issues? Many passionately disagree with court rulings:

* 77% of Americans disapproved of removing a monument to the Ten Commandments from public display in government buildings.

* 90% approve of having "In God We Trust" on our coins.

* 78% want "non-denominational prayer at public school ceremonies."

* 84% want the phrase "one nation, under God" left in the Pledge of Allegiance (while only 15% wanted it removed).[98]

The federal judicial system, in the person of a few radical judges, has ruled that displaying the Ten Commandments violates the Constitution's ban on government endorsement of religion. Where in the world do they get their ideas?

THE AGENDA
OF THE ACLU

Maybe we should look to the American Civil Liberties Union (ACLU) for answers. The ACLU has been at the forefront of the fight to remove references to God and eliminate our Christian heritage. This group has tried to position itself as an organization concerned with preserving our American freedoms. But from an historic and Biblical perspective, they have done the opposite.

Their founder, Roger Baldwin, once stated his personal philosophy: "I am for socialism, disarmament, and ultimately for abolishing the state itself as an instrument of violence and compulsion. I seek social ownership of property, the abolition of the propertied class, and sole control by those who produce wealth. Communism is the goal."[99]

The ACLU has an agenda. This includes the legalization of homosexual marriages and removal of the Bible and any Christian symbols or content from American life. Here are just a few of their more recent "causes":

* The ACLU has fought aggressively to legalize homosexual marriages.

* Even knowing that the Internet is filled with pornography, the ACLU has fought efforts to limit the access of children to this content, even forbidding parents to control what their children see.

* The ACLU has argued that the Boy Scouts of America was a "religious organization" and forced them to change their oath.

* The ACLU has fought for "peer to peer" training which would allow school officials (or others) to teach children to reject the Christian beliefs they have been taught by their parents.

* The ACLU has fought to eliminate parents' rights to be able to approve or disapprove their children from having abortions.

* The ACLU has argued that child pornography is protected by the First Amendment.[100]

This organization has made it clear it believes its interpretations and agenda are more important than the will of the American people. For example, when Alaska passed a constitutional amendment protecting marriage between one man and one woman, an ACLU executive stated, "Today's results prove that certain fundamental issues should not be left up to a majority vote."

TWISTING THE CONSTITUTION

Lino Graglio, professor of law at the University of Texas has commented on how the ACLU has taken liberties that the

Founding Fathers never imagined, encouraging this era of active judges to interpret (and reinterpret) laws and the Constitution. Graglio said, "Judge-made constitutional law is the product of judicial review...Thomas Jefferson warned that judges, always eager to expand their jurisdiction, would 'twist and shape' the Constitution 'as an artist shapes a ball of wax.' That is exactly what has happened."[101]

Unlike our Founding Fathers, many people today have rejected a belief in God, placing their faith in themselves, their feelings, their thoughts, and their "gods."

In 1995, a judge in Texas directed that no students would be allowed to mention Jesus Christ in a graduation prayer. Here was his threat: "If any student offends this court, that student will be summarily arrested and will face up to six months incarceration in the Galveston County Jail for contempt of court...Anyone who violates these orders, no kidding, is going to wish that he or she had died as a child when this court gets through with it."[102]

This judge, like so many others, was determined to "twist and shape" the Constitution in his own image. To deny history. To deny the words, warnings, and lifestyles of our Founding Fathers.

The ACLU has been on an intense campaign to remove any symbols that link America's cities, states, and national government with Christianity. It has been successful in getting religious symbols removed from the seals of Stow, Ohio; Redlands, California; Duluth, Minnesota; Plattsmouth, Nebraska; and Republic, Missouri.

The ACLU uses the threat of expensive lawsuits to intimidate government and school officials. And then they cover up their actions with nice-sounding words.[103] Anyone who speaks up (like I am in this book!) faces the possibility of being accused of bigotry. We can be persecuted in the courts, the press, and through the IRS.

To organizations like the ACLU, America's history no longer matters, nor do the views of the American people. The only thing that seems to matter is *their* belief system, *their* radical agenda, and *their* determination to remake America in *their* image without God. In the process, this organization is determined to wipe out our Christian heritage and foundation.

PROTECTION FROM TYRANNY?

It is no accident that the assaults on our laws and the Constitution have taken place at a time when belief in God and the Bible both are under attack.

Unlike our Founding Fathers, many people today have rejected a belief in God, placing their faith in themselves, their feelings, their thoughts, and their "gods." Like the ACLU, they have their own agenda and their own beliefs. Unlike our forefathers, who sought to protect us *from* tyranny, these forces have embraced authoritarian techniques of tyranny to erase our Christian heritage and history.

Organizations like the ACLU have fought to keep Americans from being able to talk about God openly or even pray and witness. Quite a contrast with our Founding Fathers! They felt the opposite, even ridiculing those who did not believe in Him. John Adams thought so little of atheists that he wrote Thomas Jefferson, "Government has no Right to hurt a hair of the head of an Atheist for his Opinions. Let him have a care of his Practices."[104]

Instead of being committed to obeying Almighty God and His Word, the goal of the ACLU is to force *their* agenda on America and reinterpret laws, the Constitution, and the Word of God to satisfy their subjective, personal opinions. While God made man in His image (Genesis 1:26), they have decided to remake God, and America in *their* image. Instead of trusting in the Bible, they trust in *their* philosophies, political doctrines, and other manmade concepts. Rather than seeking God's Kingdom, they remove Him from their world and seek a kingdom that exalts man without God.

By rejecting our solid foundation of God and His Word, Americans have embraced relativism, a world in which morals and beliefs are redefined, and absolute Truths are repudiated. The consequence is that our nation has rejected righteousness.

For America to return to righteousness and hold back God's hand of judgment and our destruction, we must...

* Return to God. Not just a belief in the Almighty but with a true hunger to know Him and a commitment to serve Him and keep His Word.

* Return to a Christ-centered, Bible-based foundation.

* Stop focusing on humanism, relativism, and human philosophies and submit to God's Word.

* Stop reinterpreting the Bible to satisfy our own selfish desires and instead, seek to conform our lives to God's purposes by being committed to His Word and surrendered to His will (Romans 12:1-2).

* Seek first His Kingdom and His righteousness (Matthew 6:33).

UNCHANGING PRINCIPLES

God is a loving God who wants the best for all of us. But He also is holy. He established laws, rules, and principles by which we need to live. And He determined the consequences of violating those rules. His Word tells us that He is jealous, and we are to have no other gods before Him (Exodus 20:4-5).

The prophet Malachi was given great insights into God's nature and the consequences for those who violate His Word. The Lord said that He does not change (Malachi 3:1-10). We need to underscore this fact and remember it always.

It should cause us to quake in our boots when we remember that we serve the same holy God who sent judgment upon Sodom and Gomorrah, who judged Israel when they turned their back on Him, and who sent His people into exile when they habitually disobeyed His Word.

Malachi warned of God's judgment:

> But who can endure the day of His coming? And who can stand when He appears? For He is like a refiner's fire and like fullers' soap; He will sit as a refiner and purifier of silver, and He will purify the priests, the sons of Levi, and refine them like gold and silver, that they may offer to the Lord offerings in righteousness (3:2-3).

After this purifying, *"then will the offering of Judah and Jerusalem be pleasing to the Lord as in the days of old and as in ancient years"* (verse 3).

But this was not the end of His authority to judge. God promises to take action against those who serve other gods, who violate His laws, who oppress others, and who act without mercy or righteousness:

Then I will draw near to you for judgment; I will be a swift witness against the sorcerers, against the adulterers, against the false swearers, and against those who oppress the hireling in his wages, the widow and the fatherless, and who turn aside the temporary resident from his right and fear not Me, says the Lord of hosts (verse 5).

But in the midst of this focus on judgment, God provided an insight into His own nature and the purpose of His actions: *"For I am the Lord, I do not change; that is why you, O sons of Jacob, are not consumed"* (verse 6).

Remember, God does not change. He desires to bless us, not judge us. Also, His eternal standards remain the same. He offers us a consistent standard and the promise of the clear choice of blessings or judgment. If we obey Him, we will reap the blessings. If we disobey, we will reap the consequences. The choice is up to us. And if we drift away, God says, *"Return to me."* When we respond to His invitation and return to Him, He promises, *"I will return to you"* (verse 7). This is the Father's Covenant with us.

God desires for us to be a people who respect and keep His Law. As a nation, we must return to the principles He provided for the moral foundation of our country and recommit to the Truth that *His* laws are the foundation for *our* laws.

Chapter Fifteen

OUR CHOICES

TODAY, WE CELEBRATE THE FREEDOMS WE HAVE AS a democracy. But for how long? As Christians, we can rejoice in the liberty God has given us. Yes, we are free to choose, but through our choices we also determine the results we will receive.

The principle is simple: We reap what we sow (Galatians 6:7).

In our democracy, we are offered many options. We make choices through our votes and also through what we choose to do with our time, talent, and treasure.

We can learn what to expect by looking at individuals in the Bible and seeing the choices they made. In every case, people were asked to choose. And the results they received were based on the decisions they made.

Joshua stood before the children of Israel and said:

> *Choose for yourselves today whom you will serve: whether the gods which your fathers served which were beyond the River, or the gods of the Amorites in whose land you are living; but as for me and my house, we will serve the LORD* (Joshua 24:15).

Jesus called to a young man and gave him a choice: *"One thing you lack: go and sell all you possess and give to the poor, and you will have treasure in heaven; and come, follow Me"* (Mark 10:21).

Sometimes people made the wrong choices and suffered the consequences:

* **Adam and Eve** made the first wrong choice, believing the serpent and disbelieving God.

* **The 12 spies** who were sent to investigate the Promised Land had choices regarding how they viewed this territory and what they would report back to the people (Numbers 13). Ten made the wrong choice about what to believe and brought back a negative, fearful report. Both they and the children of Israel paid the price by remaining in the wilderness for 40 years, and those ten spies never received the reward of entering into the land God had promised them. (Joshua and Caleb, on the other hand, were the two spies who returned with a positive report. They had the faith to believe their God was more than able to deliver the people of Canaan into their hands, and they eventually entered the land of milk and honey!)

* **Moses** made the wrong choice when he struck the rock instead of speaking to it, as God had commanded (Numbers 20:11). As a result, he never entered the Promised Land.

* **Samson** made the wrong decision when he gave in to the temptations of Delilah and told her the secret to his strength (Judges 16).

* **David** found that his life changed forever when he made the wrong choice to commit adultery with Bathsheba and have her husband killed (2 Samuel 11).

* **Judas** made the wrong decision when he betrayed Jesus (Matthew 26-27).

* **Peter** made the wrong choice when he denied he knew Jesus (Matthew 26:75).

* **The skeptics** in Athens made the wrong decision when they rejected Paul's message (Acts 17).

But some made the *right* choice and received God's *blessings:*

* **Noah** believed God and built the ark. As a result, he and his family were spared when God sent the flood (Genesis 6).

* **Abraham** obeyed God's command to leave his homeland and go on a journey, even though he didn't know the destination. Along the way, he was given the opportunity to make many other choices, but he realized the decisions he made would determine the outcome. He made right choices and so became the father of his people and the "father of faith" (Genesis 13-17).

* **Daniel** decided to stay faithful in a pagan culture where his life was threatened, and God exalted his position with the king (Daniel 1-6).

* **Esther** decided to risk her life and confront the King on behalf of her people. As a result, God saved the Jews from destruction, and His justice brought the death of their oppressor (Esther 2-9).

* **Jeremiah** made a decision to speak out and deliver God's Word to His generation, even though his life was in danger (Jeremiah 20).

* **James, John, Peter, and Andrew** made the right choice in answering the call to follow Jesus (Matthew 4:18-21).

* **A jailer** in Philippi made the right decision when he called on the name of the Lord. As a result, both he and his entire household were saved (Acts 16).

Just as we make choices and receive the consequences—for good or for bad—of our decisions, the same principle holds true for nations.

THE CHOICES OF GOD'S PEOPLE

The Bible tells us the sad story of Israel's history. At times, they were faithful and dedicated themselves to obeying God. They sought to live according to His laws and principles. They desired to serve Him and were diligent to seek Him.

Although they wavered in their commitment to Him, God remained the same and so did His laws and promises. He brought them rewards, protection, and blessings when they obeyed. But when they disobeyed Him they experienced His judgment.

Think about the moment when the people in Jerusalem gathered for the dedication of the Temple of Solomon. It was surely a dream come true. God's Promises had been fulfilled, and they seemed to be at the beginning of an era of greatness, prosperity, and power.

Solomon's father, David, had been a warrior and led them in battles of conquest that had left the kingdom secure. It seemed like nothing was impossible and that nothing could deter them from receiving God's fullest blessings.

When the Temple was dedicated, *"the cloud filled the house of the LORD, so that the priests could not stand to minister because of the cloud, for the glory of the LORD filled the house of the*

LORD" (1 Kings 8:10-11). This was a powerful confirmation that Almighty God was pleased.

People throughout the world acknowledged God's Presence and blessing. They recognized Solomon's wisdom. They came to honor him and learn more about how these people had overcome incredible odds and received such Divine favor. But the Israelites could not have known that this was the high point in their history, nor did they know they would be led on their downhill slide by Solomon himself.

> Just as we make choices and receive the consequences for our decisions, the same principle holds true for nations.

The Bible says Solomon *"loved many foreign women"* (1 Kings 11:1) and ignored God's command: *"You shall not associate with them, nor shall they associate with you, for they will surely turn your heart away after their gods."* But Solomon, even though he knew what God had commanded him, ignored His warnings. Instead, he *"held fast to these in love"* (verse 2).

Solomon's indiscretions grew more extreme as *"he had seven hundred wives, princesses, and three hundred concubines."* These women had a profound impact on his life and *"turned his heart away"* (verse 3). He even *"went after Ashtoreth the goddess of the Sidonians and after Milcom the detestable idol of the Ammonites"* (verse 5).

Then something unthinkable happened:

> *Solomon did what was evil in the sight of the LORD, and did not follow the LORD fully, as David his father had done. Then Solomon built a high place for Chemosh the detestable idol of Moab, on the mountain which is east of Jerusalem, and for Molech the detestable idol of the sons of Ammon. Thus also he did for all his foreign wives, who burned incense and sacrificed to their gods* (verses 7-8).

Solomon did not realize he would pay a heavy price for his actions and *"the LORD was angry with Solomon because his heart was turned away from the LORD."* He had no excuses. God had *"appeared to him twice, and had commanded him concerning this thing"* (verses 9-10).

Solomon had turned his back on God and no longer sought to live in righteousness. As a consequence, he was condemned to experience the fruit of his decisions. Both he and Israel suffered as the kingdom was divided into the northern kingdom (Israel) and southern kingdom (Judah). And God's people never regained the glory of those early years of his reign.

Did the children of Israel learn from Solomon's example? Yes and no.

There were seasons when they returned to righteousness and made a wholehearted commitment to God. But these periods of commitment never lasted more than a short time.

God sent mighty prophets to remind His people about His Word and the need to stand for righteousness. The northern kingdom had terrible leaders, like Ahab, who *"did evil in the sight of the Lord"* and encouraged immorality and idolatry (1 Kings 16-22).

His marriage to Jezebel is a classic example of God's people choosing to do the very thing God has warned them against doing. The consequence of Ahab's choice was that this evil woman from Sidon fostered a spirit of idolatry throughout the land, and once again, God's people turned their back on Him.

God was patient with this northern kingdom of Israel for a time, but eventually they experienced His judgment, and they were overtaken by Assyria and taken captive into that country.

Judah sought God for periods in their history. They enjoyed a revival during the reign of Asa who *"did what was right in the sight of the LORD."* He removed the idols and male cult prostitutes (1 Kings 15), and the southern kingdom made a new commitment to serve God, and He brought deliverance and victory.

Jehoshaphat, Asa's son, also *"took delight in the ways of the Lord"* (2 Chronicles 17:6). God's blessings returned and *"the dread of the LORD was on all the kingdoms of the lands which were around Judah, so that they did not make war against Jehoshaphat"* (verse 10).

But Jehoram, Jesoshaphat's son, did *not* walk in the ways of the Lord, and Judah began falling away again. Ahaziah, who succeeded Jehoram, also *"did evil in the sight of the Lord"* (2 Chronicles 22:4) but *his* son, Joash, returned Judah to Godly worship. However, in his later years, Joash, too, let Judah slide back into idolatry. Nor did Amaziah, son of Joash, have *"a loyal heart,"* and he also turned away from following God (2 Chronicles 25).

After years of walking apart from God, Judah returned to God-centered worship under Hezekiah, who restored Temple worship, kept the feasts as the Lord had directed, and led the people to recommit themselves wholeheartedly to the Almighty (chapters 29-32).

Yet his son, Manasseh, led Judah into terrible sins, and *his* son, Amon, was just as bad (chapter 33). Amon's son, Josiah, rediscovered the Law and returned Judah to God-centered worship (chapters 34-35). But Judah quickly slid into decay, and within a matter of years, Jerusalem and the Temple were destroyed, and Judah was taken into captivity by Persia.

After their return from exile, the Jews had a period of renewed commitment under the leadership of Ezra and

Nehemiah. Yet there is no indication that these "revivals" were long-lasting.

WHAT HAVE WE LEARNED?

Millions of people in America have read these stories from the Bible. Many of us are aware of Israel's blessings when they trusted in God...and we know what happened when they chose to go their own way. But the sad truth is that while Christianity still may be recognized as a dominant religion in our nation today, many are saying that we have become a "post-Christian" society.

This means we're living like a nation that *was* Christian and that *once knew* the Bible. But when it's been time to make choices, we consistently have chosen to ignore the warnings of Scripture and instead have decided to follow Israel into sin and reject the counsel of God.

What went wrong? Let me give you two powerful reasons we're in trouble:

1. We are reaping what we have sown into the lives of our children.

The Bible clearly says, *"Train up a child in the way he should go, even when he is old he will not depart from it"* (Proverbs 22:6). This is exactly what we have done. But our training has not been in Godliness and Righteousness, the Truth and Christianity. Instead, we've allowed our children to be raised in a spirit of pleasure and selfishness, rebellion and independence.

Paul told Timothy, *"The things which you have heard from me in the presence of many witnesses, entrust these to faithful men who will be able to teach others also"* (2 Timothy 2:2). However, we haven't followed this principle in our homes, and too many Christians have not been faithful parents.

I was blessed to grow up in a home filled with the Bible. I was taught the principles of Christianity from the time I was a child. Yet as I matured, my parents also tried to give me enough freedom to make my own choices. But with my freedom came boundaries I knew I couldn't cross and consequences that would occur if I did.

How many parents today are setting these kinds of parameters for their children? Instead, we've raised a generation of young people who do whatever they want. If they *do* believe in God, they want to do so on their own terms.

If we are going to turn America around, we need strong parents – moms and dads who are willing to say to their children, "You won't speak this way…dress this way…act this way."

2. Sin is abounding, and lawlessness is increasing.

As a result of our iniquity, the darkness is growing darker. This may seem impossible, since we know darkness can't exist in the presence of light, and darkness can only get darker if the light doesn't shine.

But, this is exactly what is happening in our country. Jesus said we are the *"light of the world"* (Matthew 5:14), and we have the power to dispel darkness. All we have to do is let our Light shine. But sadly, the Church too often has been silent, apathetic, and complacent.

Instead of drawing closer to the Truth and righteousness, we have fallen further away, and our Light is becoming dimmer and dimmer, not brighter and brighter. And we typically don't take action until something starts to negatively impact us and it's too late.

Well, things *are* late! And the darkness *is* impacting us!

In the past, we've responded to crisis with courage and determination, and we've turned to God for His guidance and protection. He has seen us through wars and disasters, tragedies and struggles.

As the people of God, we need to return to righteousness first.

Even when our nation has observed others in trouble, we've not been afraid to do what we felt was right. We've had Presidents who saw that we could not let happen to us what was taking place in Europe. This is why we needed to become involved in World War I and World War II. What would have been the outcome if the U.S. had not entered these conflicts? And after Pearl Harbor, there was real concern that the Japanese would invade our mainland. We *had* to get involved, and when we did, God blessed our actions.

But today's America is radically different:

* Millions of our children don't know the Word of God.

* Many of our churches are not teaching the Truth.

* Many of our schools are teaching that the Bible is fiction.

* Our courts are banning Christian symbols and sanctioning homosexual marriages.

* Countless parents are weak and ineffective.

* Our media is pumping out godlessness.

Yes, God still cares for America, but will He answer the next time we call on Him?

Will we learn from the lessons of history and the Bible? Will we repeat the mistakes of Judah and Israel? Will we realize we're headed for judgment....unless we repent and change? Will we boldly take a stand for righteousness?

Many people don't think we will. According to a recent poll, only 22% believe "America learns from its mistakes and avoids repeating them."[105] Are they right? Will we learn?

God holds us accountable. Our revivals of the past will not save us. Our history will not save us. Nor will our Founding Fathers. As the people of God, we need to return to righteousness *first*. We must humble ourselves, pray, and seek His face. Only then will a fresh move of God descend to heal our land.

Being "set apart" is
not a guaranteed path
automatically leading to
God's favor. Obedience
is required.

Chapter Sixteen

CYCLES AND PATTERNS

THE CHOICES WE HAVE BEEN DISCUSSING ARE AT THE very heart of God's plan for His people, His Church, our nation, and the world.

As you study Scripture, it becomes clear there is a distinct pattern at work regarding how the Lord deals with us. It is a cycle of obedience and blessing, disobedience and judgment. If we listen, repent, obey, humble ourselves, and cry out to God, He promises to hear, forgive, heal, restore, bless, and prosper us.

This is a crucial lesson America must learn. How much longer can the Almighty look down and tolerate the immorality of our perverse culture before He says, "Enough is enough!" and orders judgment?

For a moment, let's turn back the clock to the time God chose a man, Abraham, and destined through him to raise up a people to call His own – a seed through whom the Messiah would one day be born. The purpose of the Almighty was to demonstrate who He was and to establish His great name.

Then when the Israelites were slaves in Egypt, God intervened on their behalf and delivered them out of bondage for many reasons, but two are specifically mentioned: (1) To show the world and its leaders (Pharaoh in this instance) God's mighty power and (2) so His name would be high and lifted up. Scripture records, *"But, indeed, for this reason I have allowed you to remain, in order to show you My power and in order to proclaim My name through all the earth"* (Exodus 9:16).

In God's sight, there is a clear separation between the world and His chosen people. Scripture tells us, *"...the LORD makes a distinction between Egypt and Israel"* (Exodus 11:7). The Almighty said, *"Thus you are to be holy to Me, for I the LORD am holy; and I have set you apart from the peoples to be Mine"* (Leviticus 20:26).

PEAKS AND VALLEYS

However, being "set apart" is not a guaranteed path automatically leading to God's favor. Obedience is required. If we faithfully follow His commands, we are blessed; if we choose to disobey, there are consequences.

Nehemiah 9 recounts the story of the reoccurring patterns and cycles of God and His people. Reading it is like climbing to the peak of the mountaintop and descending to the depth of the valley – and then ascending to the mountain top again:

* *You are the Lord God.*

* *You chose Abraham.*

* *You saw the affliction of Your people in Egypt.*

* *You heard their cry, performed signs and wonders, and delivered them.*

* *You led with a pillar of cloud and fire.*

* *You spoke and gave them laws.*

* You provided them with food, water, and everything else they needed.

* They acted arrogantly and did not listen to your commandments.

* They made another god for themselves.

* In Your great compassion You did not forsake Your children.

* You cared for them in the wilderness for 40 years, and their clothes didn't wear out.

* They took possession of the land.

* You made them as numerous as the stars in Heaven, fulfilling your promise to Abraham.

* You subdued their enemies before their very eyes.

* They took possession of cities, fertile land, and every good thing.

* They ate, were filled, grew fat, and reveled in Your great goodness.

* They became disobedient and rebelled against God.

* They killed Your prophets who admonished their wicked ways.

* You delivered them into the hand of their oppressors.

* When they cried out to You, You heard and had compassion on them.

* You sent them deliverers.

* As soon as they had "rest," they committed evil again.

* Then they cried out to You once more.

Over and over, God rescued the Israelites and had compassion on their plight. This cycle repeated itself many times.

We see the same sequence in the book of Judges as the Lord sent prophets to warn the people – admonishing them to turn back to God. When they listened and obeyed, they experienced deliverance, peace, and victory over their adversaries. However, when they became "comfortable" and complacent, they forgot the Lord and disobeyed His commandments. As a result, judgment returned once more.

When the sons of Israel *"did evil in the sight of the Lord,"* God sold them into the hands of the Philistines (Judges 10:7). It was only when they acknowledged their sins and truly repented that restoration was theirs.

As I noted in the previous chapter, this same principle is evident in the pattern of leadership succession in the Old Testament. Good kings were replaced by evil kings – and as a result, blessings were often followed by tragic consequences.

Our obedience and right choices yield favor and abundance. Disobedience and wrong, willful choices bring judgment designed to draw us back to God through repentance and a renewed zeal to live for Him.

PROGRESSIVE PUNISHMENT

What happens if we fail to obey? What are the consequences of continuing to be "children of disobedience," living outside of God's laws? There is a progression of the Father's judgment and punishment. We love to hear and dwell on the promises of God, yet there are conditions to His blessings. Let me remind you, there is *always* a conditional "if" involved – as we find in this marvelous passage:

If you walk in My statutes and keep My commandments so as to carry them out, then I shall give you rains
in their season, so that the land will yield its produce and
the trees of the field will bear their fruit. Indeed, your
threshing will last for you until grape gathering, and grape
gathering will last until sowing time.

You will thus eat your food to the full and live securely
in your land. I shall also grant peace in the land, so that
you may lie down with no one making you
tremble. I shall also eliminate harmful beasts
from the land, and no sword will pass
through your land.

> Our obedience
> and right choices
> yield favor and
> abundance.

But you will chase your enemies and they
will fall before you by the sword; five of you
will chase a hundred, and a hundred of you will chase ten
thousand, and your enemies will fall before you by the
sword. So I will turn toward you and make you fruitful and
multiply you, and I will confirm My covenant with you.

You will eat the old supply and clear out the old
because of the new. Moreover, I will make My dwelling
among you, and My soul will not reject you. I will also walk
among you and be your God, and you shall be My people.

I am the LORD your God, who brought you out of the
land of Egypt so that you would not be their slaves, and I
broke the bars of your yoke and made you walk erect
(Leviticus 26: 3-13).

Then what follows is an example of the progression and
severity of God's judgment. There are seven things the Lord
said would befall His people as a direct result of their blatant
disobedience:

But *if* you do not obey Me and do not carry out all
these commandments, if, instead, you reject My statutes,

and if your soul abhors My ordinances so as not to carry out all My commandments, and so break My covenant, I, in turn, will do this to you (Leviticus 26:14-17):

1. I will appoint over you a sudden terror (verse 16).
2. You will experience sickness (verse 16).
3. You will suffer fever that will waste away the eyes and cause the soul to pine away (verse 16).
4. You will sow your seed uselessly, for your enemies will eat it up (verse 16).
5. I will set My face against you so that you will be struck down before your enemies (verse 17).
6. Those who hate you will become your rulers (verse 17).
7. You will flee even when no one is in pursuit (verse 17).

If the Israelites failed to abandon their wicked ways and adhere to God's commands, seven *additional* punishments would be theirs:

If also after these things you do not obey Me, then I will punish you seven times more for your sins. I will also break down your pride of power; I will also make your sky like iron and your earth like bronze.

Your strength will be spent uselessly, for your land will not yield its produce and the trees of the land will not yield their fruit (verses 18-20).

But wait! There's more. If they continued their sinful living, even more punishments awaited them:

If then, you act with hostility against Me and are unwilling to obey Me, I will increase the plague on you seven times according to your sins. I will let loose among you the beasts of the field, which will bereave you of your children and destroy your cattle and reduce your number so that your roads lie deserted (verses 21-22).

You may question, "Isn't this enough? Would God really continue to pour out punishment to the man or woman who disobeys?" Evidently He would, seven times more!

*And **if** by these things you are not turned to Me, but act with hostility against Me, then I will act with hostility against you; and I, even I, will strike you seven times for your sins.*

I will also bring upon you a sword which will execute vengeance for the covenant; and when you gather together into your cities, I will send pestilence among you, so that you shall be delivered into enemy hands.

When I break your staff of bread, ten women will bake your bread in one oven, and they will bring back your bread in rationed amounts, so that you will eat and not be satisfied (verses 23-25).

Will the increasing level of punishment ever end? According to the Word, if disobedience continues, there will be an additional seven penalties.

*Yet **if** in spite of this you do not obey Me, but act with hostility against Me, then I will act with wrathful hostility against you, and I, even I, will punish you seven times for your sins.*

Further, you will eat the flesh of your sons and the flesh of your daughters you will eat. I then will destroy your high places, and cut down your incense altars, and heap your remains on the remains of your idols, for My soul shall abhor you. I will lay waste your cities as well and will make your sanctuaries desolate, and I will not smell your soothing aromas.

I will make the land desolate so that your enemies who settle in it will be appalled over it. You, however, I will scatter among the nations and will draw out a sword after you, as your land becomes desolate and your cities become waste (verses 27-33).

There is only one way to reverse this terrible curse: Return to the Lord, and confess our iniquity and unfaithfulness (verse 40). When we do, God promises, *"I will remember My covenant with Jacob, and I will remember also My covenant with Isaac, and My covenant with Abraham as well"* (verse 42). And we know His Covenant extends to the descendants of these great men of God – to those who would be grafted into the vine (Gentiles) and made heirs of the promises of God (Romans 4:13).

Regarding this eternal Covenant, Moses told the people, *"For it is not an idle word for you; indeed it is your life"* (Deuteronomy 32:47).

HAVE WE FORGOTTEN?

Long before America was founded, God spoke words through Moses that are a snapshot of our nation today:

When you have eaten and are satisfied, you shall bless the LORD your God for the good land which He has given you.

Beware that you do not forget the LORD your God by not keeping His commandments and His ordinances and His statutes which I am commanding you today; otherwise, when you have eaten and are satisfied, and have built good houses and lived in them, and when your herds and your flocks multiply, and your silver and gold multiply, and all that you have multiplies, then your heart will become proud and you will forget the LORD your God who brought you out from the land of Egypt [the world] *out of the house of slavery"* (Deuteronomy 8:10-14).

Oh, how quickly and easily we have forgotten the sovereign hand of God which forged this nation.

CURSES AND BLESSINGS

Let me suggest you find a Bible and turn to Deuteronomy 28. Start reading from the first verse, and you will learn what you can expect...

> ...*if* you diligently obey the LORD your God, being careful to do all His commandments which I command you today, the LORD your God will set you high above all the nations of the earth. All these blessings will come upon you and overtake you if you obey the LORD your God (verses 1-2).

The next 12 verses list the incredible blessings for obedience: protection, provision, and God's favor. However, beginning with verse 15, the remaining 54 verses detail the punishment for disobedience. Notice there are more than *four times* as many curses as blessings!

Scripture is clear: Unrepentant sin separates us from God and has dire consequences:

* We are defeated before our enemies (1 Kings 8:33).

* The Heavens are closed – the Lord doesn't hear our prayers and His provision dries up (verse 35).

* Famine, pestilence, sickness, and plagues attack us (verse 37).

But God promises if we will walk in His ways and keep His commandments:

* He will extend our life (1 Kings 3:14).

* He will give us rest (1 Kings 5:4).

* We will abide in His love (John 15:10).

Men and women who hear and serve the Lord *"will end their days in prosperity and their years in pleasures"* (Job 36:11).

MAN'S WAY – OR GOD'S?

The story of Naaman the leper is especially insightful in showing us how the world often reacts to adversity – and at times even God's own people.

America would rather look to the power of government and the knowledge of education than to prayerfully seek the source of all strength and wisdom, Almighty God.

This highly respected man brought gifts to the king of Israel, hopeful of a healing, but it wasn't to be. Elisha the prophet heard of Naaman's plight and invited him to his home. On his arrival, Elisha told him to go and dip in the Jordan River seven times (2 Kings 5:10), but Naaman balked at the idea, questioning, "Why do I have to? Why must I do it your way?"

Jordan was a filthy, muddy river, so he asked, *"Are not Abanah and Pharpar, the rivers of Damascus, better than all the waters of Israel? Could I not wash in them and be clean?"* (verse 12)

However, there is a deeper meaning to this story. While Abanah and Pharpar were clear rivers, their names meant "man-made wisdom, knowledge and sufficiency." Without realizing it, Naaman was saying, "I would rather look to man than to God."

Jordan means "the River of God." It was by obedience and doing things the Lord's way – looking to the Almighty and not man – that Naaman was healed of his leprosy.

The world would much rather play by its own rules, and many in the Church seem to feel the same way. America would rather look to, and rely on, the power of government and the knowledge of education than to prayerfully seek the source of all strength and wisdom, Almighty God.

THE RESULTS OF REPENTANCE

We must never forget there are serious consequences for turning our back on our Creator.

During the reign of Hoshea, the king of Assyria captured Samaria and took Israel away into exile to Assyria. This happened because *"the sons of Israel had sinned against the LORD their God, who had brought them up from the land of Egypt"* (2 Kings 17:7). They secretly did things which were not right before God – including idol worship (verse 12). The Bible records their evil deeds:

> *They forsook all the commandments of the LORD their God and made for themselves molten images, even two calves, and made an Asherah and worshiped all the host of heaven and served Baal.*

> *Then they made their sons and their daughters pass through the fire, and practiced divination and enchantments, and sold themselves to do evil in the sight of the LORD, provoking Him* (verses 16-17).

What was God's response? The Lord was so angry, He *"gave them into the hand of plunderers, until He had cast them out of His sight"* (verse 20).

What a contrast we find later in the story of King Hezekiah (2 Kings 19). When he heard that the king of Assyria was preparing to invade Israel, he humbled himself, tore his clothes, put on sackcloth and ashes, repented and cried out to God. Because of his contrite heart, the Lord heard him and sent an angel to defeat the Assyrians. God destroyed 185,000 of the opposing army – and Israel didn't have to assemble for battle or even face their enemy!

A PROMISE AND A WARNING

We all are encouraged by the powerful verse which reads, *"If My people who are called by My name humble themselves and pray and seek My face and turn from their wicked ways, then I will hear from heaven, will forgive their sin and will heal their land"* (2 Chronicles 7:14).

However, what follows is equally important. God told Solomon...

Now My eyes will be open and My ears attentive to the prayer offered in this place. For now I have chosen and consecrated this house that My name may be there forever, and My eyes and My heart will be there perpetually (verses 15-16).

Then Solomon is issued this stern warning to the people on behalf of God:

But if you turn away and forsake My statutes and My commandments which I have set before you, and go and serve other gods and worship them, then I will uproot you from My land which I have given you, and this house which I have consecrated for My name I will cast out of My sight and I will make it a proverb and a byword among all peoples.

As for this house, which was exalted, everyone who passes by it will be astonished and say, "Why has the LORD done thus to this land and to this house?" And they will say, "Because they forsook the LORD, the God of their fathers who brought them from the land of Egypt, and they adopted other gods and worshiped them and served them; therefore He has brought all this adversity on them" (verses 19-22).

We bring Heaven's judgment and wrath on ourselves as a direct result of our continuing sin and our refusal to obey and walk in God's ways. He tells us, *"You have forsaken Me, so I also have forsaken you"* (2 Chronicles 12:5).

Could this be the reason our nation appears to be on the eve of destruction? Is there hope for America?

REBUILDING THE FOUNDATION

Our nation is at a crossroads – in large part because the people of God do not seem to know which road to choose. We have chased other gods...materialism, self-gratification, earthly pleasures, adulterous relationships, alcohol, drugs, and complacency. Where is the line of demarcation between the world and the Church?

The psalmist David asked, *"If the foundations are destroyed, what can the righteous do?"* (Psalm 11:3).

> Our nation is at a crossroads – in large part because the people of God do not seem to know which road to choose.

As documented earlier in this book, America was founded on Biblical principles, yet today our nation has lost its moral compass. But what about those of us who call ourselves Christians – which means to be "Christ-like"? Do we reflect Him to our culture? Or do we just blend into society without making any impact on those around us?

Another psalmist wrote:

The king is not saved by a mighty army;
A warrior is not delivered by great strength.
A horse is a false hope for victory;
Nor does it deliver anyone by its great strength.

Behold, the eye of the LORD is on those who fear Him,
On those who hope for His lovingkindness,
To deliver their soul from death
And to keep them alive in famine.
Our soul waits for the LORD;
He is our help and our shield.
For our heart rejoices in Him,
Because we trust in His holy name.
Let Your lovingkindness, O LORD, be upon us,
According as we have hoped in You.
(Psalm 33:16-22)

This very moment, the Lord is calling to His people, pleading, *"Return to Me!"*

> *For if you return to the LORD, your brothers and your sons will find compassion before those who led them captive and will return to this land. For the LORD your God is gracious and compassionate, and will not turn His face away from you if you return to Him* (2 Chronicles 30:9).

I believe as the Church of Jesus Christ goes, so goes America. If we refuse to return to righteousness, our beloved nation will continue in a downward spiral. Today, will you make a personal commitment to lead by example? If there is not a transformation, judgment will descend, and we *will* find ourselves on the Eve of Destruction.

It's not too late to cry out to God for mercy and ask Him to forgive our sin and bring restoration.

Chapter Seventeen

KINGDOM LIVING

ONE OF THE REASONS SO MANY CHURCHES AND Christians are anemic is that they don't understand the importance or relevance of Kingdom living. This is critical to living a successful, victorious Christian life and enjoying the full benefits of God's Kingdom. And it's essential to the future of our country. If America is going to survive and return to righteousness, we need to recapture the sense of living in God's Kingdom.

Many fail to realize that the Bible is a book about a King, His people, and a Kingdom. Ultimate authority, lawgiving, and even care come from the King, not His people.

We need to return to the conviction of the Pilgrims and our Founding Fathers that God was the ultimate Authority for all laws and government, and that the Bible is His Word.

Scripture makes it clear that Jesus came to bring us God's Kingdom. John was sent to prepare the way for His coming. His proclamation was simple: *"Repent, for the kingdom of heaven is at hand"* (Matthew 3:2).

Kingdom living was the focus of Jesus' message and ministry. He gave us many parables to describe what the Kingdom of Heaven was like (see Matthew 13, for example).

He told us that righteousness is central to this domain and that the Kingdom of God is not what we eat or drink, or our resources or power. Rather, it is *"righteousness, peace, and joy in the Holy Spirit"* (Romans 14:17).

Righteousness is so important because it means we acknowledge that God is our King, and we are His subjects. It also is vital because our "right living" indicates we are living in obedience to our King, serving and seeking His Kingdom.

THE CALL OF THE MASTER

Jesus told a story concerning a man who went on a journey. He left one of his servants five talents (about $1,000 in today's rate of exchange), a second two talents, and a third just one talent. The first two servants put their talents to work, but the third hid his and did nothing with it.

When the man returned, he praised the servants who had been given five and two talents because they had done something productive with what they had been given. Because of their good stewardship, the talents they had been given had literally doubled. The one who was given five talents gained five more. The one who was given two talents gained two more.

But the master condemned the servant who buried his talent, telling him that if nothing else, he should have at least put his money in the bank where it would have earned interest so that when he arrived, he would have received some interest (Matthew 25:14-30).

Through this and other parables, Jesus taught that each of us has been given responsibilities. We are to be good servants and stewards of the resources our King has given us.

KINGDOM LIVING

When you live in a kingdom, you forfeit certain rights, but you also gain others. In a kingdom, it makes no difference what you think; what matters is what the *king* thinks. Our Pilgrim forefathers understood this very well.

Many Christians today are concerned more with their *own* opinion on subjects such as abortion, homosexual marriage, and the sanctity of life. But if we want to be authentic, Bible-believing Christians, we need to be concerned with what our *King* says. This is the way His Kingdom works. He establishes the rules.

We are a people who belong first to a Kingdom, and the Kingdom of God is not a democracy. But within His Kingdom, God continually gives us choices.

It's wonderful that here in America, we live in a democracy and have the freedom to vote, speak, and do what we want...within the limits of the law, of course. But many Believers misapply the spirit and principle of democracy to God and His Kingdom.

PRACTICAL CHRISTIAN LIVING TODAY

We can't afford to put what we believe are our own personal freedoms and rights above what our King says. If we truly desire all the blessings God promises us in His Word, we need to make Him the King of our lives and live according to His Kingdom principles.

It's time to be concerned about doing the will of our King. It's time to stop focusing on our own personal desires and concerns, and commit ourselves without reservation to *His* preferences, interests, and Kingdom.

We have a "manual," a "roadmap," from God that shows us what to do and how to live. It reveals to us the principles of living in His Kingdom and, like our Constitution, sets forth our rights and the privileges. The roadmap is the Bible. Instead of being conformed to the world's systems, beliefs, and ways of doing things, we're to be transformed by the Word of God (Romans 12:2).

Countless Christians don't spend time reading and studying the Bible. It's not their "daily bread." Consequently, they don't understand what their King really says or believes. Instead of adopting His Kingdom principles, they form their own opinions. As a result, they drift further and further from who God desires for them to be as citizens of His Kingdom.

Other Believers think that because they live under grace, they can use grace as a license to do as they please. In the process, they embrace beliefs and actions contrary to God's Word. But as Paul warns, we must not use our liberty (grace) as a license to sin (Romans 6:14-16).

We can choose to love and obey God, and return to His standards of righteousness and Kingdom living, or we can choose to do things our own way. If we disobey, the pattern in the Bible strongly suggests we will suffer the consequences and experience His judgment.

How much better off will we be if we choose to submit our lives and our will to our King and to His principles of Kingdom living? If we choose to have a personal and intimate relationship with a loving God? If we choose to seek and obey Him, and live our lives as a reflection of His Kingdom's standard of righteousness? When we do, we can expect to enjoy His blessings.

Chapter Eighteen

SPIRITUAL WARFARE

HAVE YOU EVER WONDERED WHY AMERICAN HISTORY has become such a lightning rod? Why so many people have been reinterpreting our roots and superimposing their views about our Founding Fathers and our nation's legacy? Why powerful organizations are spending millions of dollars to remove Christianity from our way of life?

Think about this: We live in both a natural (or physical) world, and at the same time we live in a spiritual world.

No one can deny the fact we are engaged in a cultural war. A cultural war that questions what is right and what is wrong. No, more than that. A cultural war that says just because something is right for you, doesn't make it right for me. Everything is relevant. A cultural war that demands tolerance for everything and everyone except believers in Jesus Christ.

We are also engaged in a spiritual war. What on the surface looks like a battle of social agendas and quests for personal and political power are rooted in deeper, fundamentally spiritual issues.

In one sense, yes, we need to fight this cultural war in the physical "seen" world in which we live. We need to vote and get involved. We need to speak up and take action. We need to be agents of change and a positive influence in our society for Kingdom principles.

But more important than this is recognizing the spiritual war taking place in the "unseen" world and engaging in battle on that front.

When the Apostle Paul wrote a letter to a group of Believers in the city of Corinth, he told them,

> For though we walk in the flesh, we do not war according to the flesh, for the weapons of our warfare are not of the flesh, but divinely powerful for the destruction of fortresses. We are destroying speculations and every lofty thing raised up against the knowledge of God and we are taking every thought captive to the obedience of Christ, (2 Corinthians 10:3-5).

To what fortresses was Paul referring? Those of spiritual wickedness in heavenly places.

Approximately five or more years later, Paul was still concerned that Believers understood the significance of where the real battle was taking place. So he sent another letter to a group of Believers in the ancient city of Ephesus. He wrote, "For our struggle is not against flesh and blood, but against the rulers, against the powers, against the world forces of this darkness, against the spiritual forces of wickedness in the heavenly places" (Ephesians 6:12).

Please pay close attention to this: Every spiritual force manifests itself in a physical form and every physical manifestation has its root in a spiritual force.

It's vitally important that we win the cultural war. Even more important is that we win the spiritual war. The battle begins with each one of us. Each of us needs to live our lives reflecting the principles of our King and His Kingdom. And as citizens of His Kingdom, we need to be daily and actively engaged in spiritual warfare.

The Bible doesn't call Believers to engage in natural warfare, but in spiritual warfare. The purpose of my book isn't to present an in-depth study of war in the spiritual realm. But some understanding is necessary to grasp what we're up against and how to do battle. So what is spiritual warfare?[106]

Spiritual warfare begins with the recognition that there are two opposing kingdoms. Some call these two kingdoms light and darkness or good and evil. The simple explanation is that these two kingdoms are God and His forces versus Satan and his. As Believers, we're citizens and residents of God's Kingdom.

A fierce battle is raging in the spiritual realm. Invisible forces have burrowed deep into the prevailing culture. They have helped shape the political, economic, and social activities of politicians and organizations. And these forces bitterly oppose our King, our Kingdom, and our mission.

That's why we need to understand Kingdom living and spiritual warfare. As citizens of God's Kingdom, we have been given delegated authority. If we expect to win the battle, we need to exercise this authority.

> Every spiritual force manifests itself in a physical form and every physical manifestation has its root in a spiritual force.

Jesus astonished the people of His time because He understood the principle of spiritual authority. He came to this earth for many reasons. One was to bring the Kingdom of Heaven and its authority and rulership back to this earth. People were amazed by His ministry. Why? Because He commanded even unclean spirits and *"they obey[ed] him"* (Mark 1:27). He knew His Father had given Him authority over *all* the power of the enemy. All Jesus had to do was exercise that authority and speak. This is delegated authority in action!

OUR REAL ENEMY

Our ancestors here in America tended to make the mistake of overemphasizing the devil. However, we're inclined to make the opposite mistake. In fact, many Christians forget that we live in a physical and spiritual world. They seem to ignore the reality that we have a very real enemy: the devil who has very real power. Most people believe there is a higher power: God. Far fewer believe there is a *literal* devil.

I wish that were true. The world would be a different place without the devil, his forces of evil, and his influence. The truth is that the devil is very real. He is a ruler. He has a kingdom. And he has servants. He knows the only sure way to destroy humanity is to sever our dependence on God and our allegiance to the Almighty.

When God created man, He gave him authority and dominion over the earth. (Genesis 1:26-28). But when man sinned in the Garden of Eden, his authority and dominion were handed over to Satan. How can we be sure? Listen to the words of the devil himself when he spoke during Jesus' temptation in the wilderness:

> And the devil said to Him, 'I will give You all this domain and its glory; **for it has been handed over to me,** and I give it to whomever I wish. Therefore if You worship before me, it shall all be Yours' (Luke 4: 6-7).

Two striking things are mentioned here by the devil. One, he said his dominion – his authority –*"has been handed over to me."* Who gave it to him? Certainly not God. No, Adam and Eve relinquished their dominion as a result of their sin and disobedience...and as a result of their desire for independence from God.

Secondly, the devil said he had the power to give his dominion to whomever he wished. Incredible! Little did he know that Christ was about to strip him of his dominion!

One of the things Jesus accomplished through His death on the Cross...His victory over death, hell, and the grave... living a sinless life...and by paying the acceptable sacrifice and penalty for our sins...was that He took back from Satan the dominion man had forfeited in the Garden.

Then he turned around and gave His authority over the devil's power to His disciples and to us today (Luke 10:19)! Jesus didn't say He gave us power over the devil. He stated He gave us *authority* over the *devil's* power. We have been deputized. We have been given delegated authority.

ULTIMATE AUTHORITY

Matthew 8 tells the story of a centurion who came to Jesus asking that his servant, who was sick at home, be healed. When Jesus offered to come and heal him, the centurion answered:

> *"Lord, I am not worthy for You to come under my roof, but just say the word, and my servant will be healed. For I also am a man under authority, with soldiers under me; and I say to this one, 'Go' and he goes, and to another, 'Come!' and he comes, and to my slave, 'Do this!' and he does it"* (Matthew 8:5-9).

How did Jesus respond? *"He marveled and said to those who were following, 'Truly I say to you, I have not found such great faith with anyone in Israel'"* (verse 10).

The centurion recognized that Jesus was a man of authority. But Christ's rule wasn't over the army of Rome. No, His authority was over sickness, disease, death, sin, and the powers of Satan. The centurion recognized this.

You and I need to understand that if we are true children of God, if we are living and walking according to His Kingdom principles, then Jesus has delegated that same authority to *us*.

Jesus told His disciples, *"Truly I say to you, whatever you bind on earth shall have been bound in heaven; and whatever you loose on earth shall have been loosed in heaven"* (Matthew 18:18).

Many Christians suffer and go through life filled with problems because they do not understand or exercise the spiritual authority they've been given. They think the devil has the power, and there is nothing they can do about it. Their lives are tossed here and there, and they feel they have no control over their circumstances.

Nothing can be further from the truth! As Believers, we need to start acting with the authority God has already given us.

One of the enemy's strategies is to influence the kinds of thoughts that enter our minds. If we entertain an idea or thought the devil has introduced, if we dwell on it and allow it to grow, we give the devil an entrance into our minds from which he will attempt to manipulate our thoughts, and ultimately, our actions.

Paul recognized this danger when he said that we must not even give the devil a foothold in our lives (Ephesians 4:27).

Instead of allowing the devil to introduce thoughts and images into our thinking, we are to submit our minds to the Lordship of Christ and His thoughts. Paul gave us these guidelines:

Finally, brethren, whatever is true, whatever is honorable, whatever is right, whatever is pure, whatever is lovely, whatever is of good repute, if there is any excellence and if anything worthy of praise, dwell on these things. The things you have learned and received and heard and seen in me, practice these things, and the God of peace will be with you (Philippians 4:8-9).

We are to take captive the thoughts the enemy wants to bring into our minds.

Paul tells us we are to cast down imaginations and every thought that is exalted *"against the knowledge of God."* We are not to let words, images, and ideas dominate our minds but to make captive, or to take prisoner, every thought to the obedience of Christ in submission to His will (2 Corinthians 10:5).

This means we're not to be passive but instead we're to make the devil's thoughts our prisoners. What do you do with those behind bars? Guard them. Keep them under lock and key. And don't let them out!

There are many devious ways the devil tries to influence, control, and shape our lives. We need to keep all of these things prisoners and never let them escape!

THE REAL BATTLE

To understand the importance of spiritual warfare, we need to be aware that the devil delights in controlling the affairs of nations, cities, households, and people. He does this through the spiritual realm…influencing what people think and meditate on and the standards by which they live.

Paul's reminder to us bears repeating:

"For our struggle is not against flesh and blood, but against the rulers, against the powers, against the world

forces of this darkness, against the spiritual forces of wickedness in the heavenly places" (Ephesians 6:12-13).

Are these rulers, powers, and forces just "located" in the *"heavenly places"* or do they have specific "assignments" over "locations" in the heavens? Daniel mentions the angel princes linked to Persia and Greece. Ezekiel references the guardian cherub associated with the king of Tyre. In Revelation John refers to Babylon as a home for demons and a haunt for every evil spirit.

Could it be that sometimes Christians come under spiritual attack simply because they have knowingly, or even unknowingly, invaded the "territory" of the devil or his demon cronies? For example, in Tibet, "territorial spirits" are not honored as guests but as lords of the soil of the continent.

> When we enter into spiritual battles, we need to remember that we wear the badge of spiritual authority.

Think of what's happened in the United States. Our Forefathers came here to find religious freedom. Despite what many in our society fail to recognize or embrace, these were Godly people who "extended" the "borders" of Christianity to our nation so that it became a predominantly God-fearing, Christ-worshiping society.

But look at America today. Because we have become the great melting pot of cultures which have brought with them their rich heritage and traditions, we also have been invaded by their gods and idol worship. Our country now has become home to millions of Hindus, Buddhists, Muslims, and members of other religions. As a result, principalities have infiltrated our territory. Spiritual strongholds have been established in our society, in our geographic regions, and in the minds of people.

"Strongholds" are created when people welcome, invite, or entertain evil and allow it to linger in their minds...in their physical locality. Knowingly and unknowingly, people enter into "pacts" with these rulers and powers. They consequently come under their "dominion" and their territorial rulership. As each successive generation maintains and continues this "servitude," the "pact" grows stronger, as does the principality's influence.

But we are not helpless in the face of these strongholds. God has given us the resources we need to break their influence over our minds, our families, our communities, our nation, and the world. The Lord has armed us with weapons to be used in offensive spiritual warfare. This power is so strong and forceful that it can destroy the works of the enemy.

ARMED WITH POWER

If we fight the demonic forces that are waging war against God's people everywhere, particularly here in the United States, we can expect to be attacked. But we do not need to be afraid. The Bible assures us, *"greater is He that is in you than he that is in the world"* (1 John 4:4).

When we enter into spiritual battles, we need to remember that we wear the badge of spiritual authority...delegated authority. Behind every policeman is the backing of the entire police force of that area, plus the FBI, the National Guard, and the Armed Forces of the United States. In the same way, supporting every Christian is the delegated authority of Jesus Christ that we have been given in the spiritual realm.

Jesus said that He sent us into the world as His ambassadors, armed with power (John 17:18). God sent His Son to this earth for a purpose: *"that He might destroy the works of the devil"* (1 John 3:8).

These evil works were the consequences that entered the world through Adam and Eve's disobedience...sin, sickness, and death. God sent His Son to earth with all AUTHORITY over ALL the power of the devil. Jesus said, *"All power is given unto me in heaven and in earth"* (Matthew 28:18).

Since Jesus was sent here by His Father with ALL authority...and since He told us that as His Father sent Him to this earth, even so He sends *us*...then we have been delegated ALL the authority that was given to Christ!

Every one of these spiritual principles applies to our personal lives. But they also apply to nations.

To be prepared and ready for the attacks of the enemy, we need to put on the whole armor of God (Ephesians 6:13-19). And we must be aware that we can be wounded if we go into battle without being prepared.

This is why we must fill our minds with the Word of God. We must be able to wield the Word like a sword, one of the many weapons of spiritual warfare we have been given and a key part of being prepared spiritually.

PEOPLE OF TRUTH

Paul wrote that we need to *"stand firm"* (Ephesians 6:13). This means we must be bold and fearless, not afraid of being condemned, criticized, or ridiculed for our faith.

There were two conditions Paul said would help us stand steadfast: *"Having girded your loins with truth, and having put on the breastplate of righteousness"* (verse 14).

First, we must be people of Truth and be surrounded by it. Our lives need to be characterized by God's Truth. We must not allow hypocrisy or deceit in anything we do. In our personal conduct, on our jobs, within our families, in our neighborhoods, or in how we choose to spend our time.

This is one of the reasons the devil continually attacks the concept of Truth. He does not want us to stand for it, because he knows that if our lives are girded with Truth, we can withstand his assaults and be victorious. With this commitment to Truth throughout our lives, we are ready to stand!

But Paul also gave a second condition: we are to put on *"the breastplate of righteousness."* This shows us the necessity of righteousness in spiritual warfare.

The best protection for our lives is a life of "right living," which only the Lord can provide. We help guard ourselves and our families from attack when we do right and obey God. Our heart (our emotions and feelings) needs to be protected by righteousness.

Paul also talked about the *"shield of faith"* (verse 16). We cannot be saved or shielded through our own actions. We need faith. This is our part in being ready to stand and defeat our enemy. If we do not arm ourselves with this shield, we will find ourselves going places and doing things that can make us vulnerable to the enemy's attacks.

To win the battle for our own lives and for America, Christians need to be on the spiritual offensive. The devil has intimidated many Christians into believing they are powerless. They are afraid to venture into situations they think are more powerful than they are. This is a lie from the pit of hell!

> **We must be able to wield the Word like a sword.**

Jesus gave us authority so we would use it. Authority against physical ailments. Against confusion. Authority against spiritual attacks. Authority over every way in which the devil wants to kill, steal, and destroy our lives (John 10:10). And He gave us this authority that we might bring down the enemy's strongholds!

WE HAVE THE RESOURCES

Many people, both Christians and non-Christians, are so confused today. But we should not be surprised. The Bible says that *"the god of this world has blinded the minds of the unbelieving"* (2 Corinthians 4:4). It's our job to open their eyes. And God has given us the power! Where the devil has…

* brought blindness, we must bring SIGHT.

* brought darkness, we must bring LIGHT.

* brought despair, we must bring HOPE.

* brought fear, we must bring FAITH.

* sown sickness, disease, and pain, we must bring HEALING.

* sown confusion, we must bring CLARITY.

* brought unrest, we must bring PEACE.

* robbed men and women of dignity, we must restore the ESTEEM in which their Heavenly Father holds them.

* brought death, we must bring LIFE!

These principles are true for us as individuals, and they are true for our country!

The devil desires to weaken America so he can keep us stumbling in darkness. He schemes to keep us from enjoying the benefits of God's Kingdom. And he conspires to prevent us from spreading the Light of the Gospel to a needy world.

But the Lord has given us the tools and resources to fight this spiritual battle and defeat the enemy's evil. Together, we can win this war. But we cannot remain indifferent or passive. We must stand! We must declare war! And we must fight!

History and the Bible demonstrate that God *will* pour out His judgment...unless we repent and return to serving Him.

Will we continue to support the goals of political correctness? Or will we decide to follow after the uncompromising, eternally true Word of God? Will we seek our own way or seek His Kingdom and His righteousness?

Today the nation of Israel remains in a precarious situation, surrounded by her enemies and vastly outnumbered.

Chapter Nineteen

ISRAEL AND THE MIDDLE EAST

HERE IS ONE SIGNIFICANT REASON SATAN IS SO EAGER to ravage America and weaken our commitment to Christianity: our country's role in the nation of Israel and in the Middle East.

Since the beginning of history, Satan has been on a mission to destroy God's Chosen People. Throughout the Bible, we read how God's leaders and people were deceived and fell into temptation. As a result, Israel experienced judgment, death, and destruction. Evil men such as Haman and Hitler have sought continually to annihilate the Jews.

Today the nation of Israel remains in a precarious situation, surrounded by her enemies and vastly outnumbered. The forces of Satan are lined up to eliminate Israel.

America has been Israel's strongest ally. And the Jewish people and leaders have realized that Christian America is their best friend. But powerful political, economic, and spiritual forces are at work, trying to change all of that.

Just think about the economic power controlled by the

Muslim world through their oil supplies. In one respect, they hold many nations hostage and are able to raise or lower prices to reflect their own views of the world situation. And many governments have become willing to do just about anything to placate these Arab oil states. Across the globe, businesses and business leaders lobby intensely for us to cave in and do anything to accommodate Muslims.

There also have been important changes brought about by the terrorist attacks of September 11. In an effort to appease Muslims and reduce tensions and the possibility of more terrorist attacks, there have been efforts to welcome Muslims into the world community. People have felt compelled to become more tolerant toward Islam and to sugarcoat the teachings of this religion while ignoring the spiritual realities.

In the process, confusion has spread about Islam. As I noted earlier, many people today believe that the Muslim "god" is the same as the God of the Bible and of Judaism and Christianity. But this is not true.

WHAT IS THEIR AGENDA?

Muslims are not a nation with geographic boundaries. They are a nation of peoples with a common belief wherever they may geographically live. Wherever they are found, they are part of *that* kingdom. Their first allegiance is not to any particular country but to Islam.

We need to face the fact that we are being attacked by those intent on our destruction. They have an agenda. The word "Islam" itself means to "submit." This is a system, a religion, a people with an agenda which is to get us to submit or die. Their objective is world conquest.

Today, anyone who criticizes Muslims is subject to attack, even if what they say is true. Everyone seems to be hyper-sensitive to avoid saying or doing anything that might offend any Muslim. However, it seems it's politically correct to be able to speak out against and criticize the Bible or Christians without consequence. But dare to voice your opinion against the Koran or Muslims, and you are threatened with your life.

Even plays and books that criticize Islam are banned, and their authors may be forced to go into hiding.

In 2006, Pope Benedict XVI made historically accurate comments concerning Islamic history. Here was the head of the Catholic Church, doing what his predecessors and Christian leaders have done since the book of Acts: defending the faith. Talking about history. Championing its virtues. Answering its critics.

But what was the reaction? Riots broke out. Christians were shot. The pope himself was threatened with assassination. And he was pressured to back down and apologize.[107]

What's wrong with this picture? Have we become so afraid of radical Muslims that we will not speak the Truth?

While we clearly disagree with Muslims and the claims of Islam, one thing we can admire is their commitment. In fact, the world could be won for Christ if Christians had the same dedication and drive to serve God and His Kingdom!

We need to stop being afraid to speak the truth concerning Islam. Although it's true that we need to show them the love of Christ, we cannot give into weakness or compromise.

OUR ONLY HOPE

Many today are focused on the political, economic, and military threats posed by the Muslim world. But God wants us to realize that our greatest and only defense is to return to righteousness. To return to Him!

Are we afraid of Muslims? Atheists? Demonic forces? Are we afraid to speak the Truth? Our only hope is that we stop running and start bravely fighting.

God will continue to bless America as long as God's people in this nation remain committed to Him, remain committed to humbling ourselves, praying, seeking His face, turning from our wicked ways...**and as long as we stand by Israel.**

The Lord loves His people. And He promises to bless those who stand by them, support them, and pray for them. The Bible commands us, *"Pray for the peace of Jerusalem: May they prosper who love you"* (Psalm 122:6). Scripture also tells us that those who touch Israel touch *"the apple of His eye"* (Zechariah 2:8). God is clear when He says He will bless those who bless Israel and curse those who curse Israel (Genesis 12:3).

How we respond to the Jewish people is a sign to God. Will we, as a nation, turn our back on His people, as so many others have done throughout history, and even today?

If America is to stay free and strong, we need to stand for righteousness. We need to be people who uphold Biblical Truth, not the compromises of the world or the lies of the devil. We must be a nation that is committed to Israel.

Chapter Twenty

WHAT CAN YOU DO? PART 1

I WANT YOU TO KNOW THAT YOU HAVE AN important part to play in keeping judgment and destruction from America! How?

Just think about our history. How did America come to be based on Christian principles? Why did God send revivals and save our nation?

Over and over, He acted because His people prayed. They put into action the words that God spoke to Solomon after the Temple was completed:

> *I have heard your prayer and have chosen this place for Myself as a house of sacrifice. If I shut up the heavens so that there is no rain, or if I command the locust to devour the land, or if I send pestilence among My people, and My people who are called by My name humble themselves and pray and seek My face and turn from their wicked ways, then I will hear from heaven, will forgive their sin and will heal their land (2 Chronicles 7:12-14).*

The Lord was telling Solomon that the responsibility for His intervention in the world was on His people. As much as

God hated sin and the iniquity on earth, He was not waiting for the wicked to stop being wicked. He did not require that unrighteousness, idolatry, or other forms of sin should be halted in the world by the ungodly.

No, He looked to His people to take action. *They* were the ones who needed to humble themselves. *They* needed to pray and seek His face. *They* needed to turn from their wicked ways.

The same principle applies in our lives today.

As He did in the time of Noah, Abraham, Solomon, Joshua, Daniel, Ezra, and Paul, God looks at humanity filled with sin and wickedness. Are things bad enough for Him to send judgment? Has evil become so widespread that He must take action? If so, what measures will He take? What kind of judgment will He send? Upon whom will it fall?

While we don't know the answers to these questions, we *do* know God is looking to His people to determine whether or not He will send judgment.

Also, based on the promise He made to Solomon, He also depends upon us to determine whether or not He sends rain or spares the land from economic or natural disasters.

So the first thing you can do to bring about change is pray!

When you come before the Lord in prayer, come in humility. Ask Him to show you things in your life that displease Him. Any thoughts, habits, actions, emotions, or speech that are contrary to the life He wants you to live.

Then ask Him to forgive you and to help you repent. To repent means to change the way you're thinking…change the way you're doing things…to make a turnaround and go a different direction. When you do, you'll find God's promise will be true: *"Then I will hear from heaven and will forgive their sin and heal their land"* (2 Chronicles 7:14).

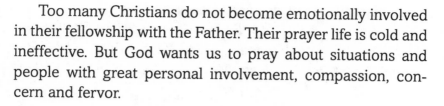

Too many Christians do not become emotionally involved in their fellowship with the Father. Their prayer life is cold and ineffective. But God wants us to pray about situations and people with great personal involvement, compassion, concern and fervor.

It's time for Christians to seek the Lord with intensity and feeling. Jesus said, *"From the days of John the Baptist until now the kingdom of heaven suffers violence, and violent men take it by force"* (Matthew 11:12). It's not time for timid "now I lay me down to sleep" prayers!

James 5:16 tells us, *"The effectual fervent prayer of a righteous man avails much."* To be fervent means to be "red hot." To be righteous is to "be in right standing." If we want our prayers to be answered, we must be spiritually (not physically) violent. We need to have an "on fire" prayer life. We need to approach the Almighty with force and conviction. We must remain persistent until God answers!

Did you know He actually *wants* us to pray this way?

PRAYING WITH PERSISTENCE

All of us know what it means to be discouraged or feel defeated. Sometimes we can feel like failures...like we have fallen short of the mark or have been a disappointment to God. In practical and spiritual terms, each of us must decide if we will give in to these feelings *or* if we will persevere and take these thoughts captive (2 Corinthians 10:5).

When faced with circumstances in our lives that seem impossible to overcome, the devil wants us to be doubtful, afraid, worried, discouraged, or lose heart. Often when people don't experience an answer to their prayers, the devil will come to them and plant a lie in their minds. He'll tell them, "God isn't listening. He doesn't care. You've done something wrong! You're being punished!"

Don't believe these lies! To teach us how we should continue to pray, even when we don't see the answer to our prayers, Jesus told a story about a widow and an unjust judge in which He describes that it's possible, and even likely, that at some point, we will lose heart, be discouraged, and even consider giving up hope.

However, the Lord uses this story to teach us how we can *prevent* these feelings...how *not* to lose heart...*not* to be discouraged... *not* to give up hope. Through the following parable, He's telling us, "Don't stop believing. Don't stop asking." Here's what He said to do when we feel like giving up:

Then He spoke a parable to them, that men always ought to pray and not lose heart, saying: "There was in a certain city a judge who did not fear God nor regard man. Now there was a widow in that city; and she came to him, saying, 'Get justice for me from my adversary.'

"And he would not for a while; but afterward he said within himself, 'Though I do not fear God nor regard man, yet because this widow troubles me I will avenge her, lest by her continual coming she weary me.'"

Then the Lord said, "Hear what the unjust judge said. And shall God not avenge His own elect who cry out day and night to Him, though He bears long with them? I tell you that He will avenge them speedily. Nevertheless, when the Son of Man comes, will He really find faith on the earth?" (Luke 18:1-8 NKJV)

There are three characters in this story: a widow, a judge, and the woman's adversary. Clearly, the woman represents us, and the judge depicts God. The adversary represents any organization, person, situation, need, or anyone who opposes or causes us problems. And in spiritual terms, he symbolizes the devil.

The fact that Jesus uses a widow to make His illustration is significant, because she portrays people with the least influence in society, the fewest assets, and the most problems to overcome. If a widow can find a way to conquer her *"adversaries,"* then anyone can.

When faced with opposition and opponents of various kinds, we easily can lose heart. We can become worn out and exhausted from our efforts to do what is right, confront our foes, and wage spiritual warfare. We can become utterly spiritless, discouraged, and despondent.

But Jesus says whenever we find ourselves in a state of despair, we need to take our case to the Judge! We don't need to keep our complaints and concerns to ourselves. And we certainly don't need to complain to others. We need to take our problems to God Himself!

The key to victory comes from the Judge. As long as we battle our opponents by ourselves in our own strength, we will become increasingly tired and wear ourselves out. But everything changes when we go to the Judge. The Judge, God, has the power to solve any problems you may face. He has the answers to the questions in your life. And He has not planned any defeats for you!

GETTING GOD'S ATTENTION

Jesus said that the Judge will *"avenge"* the widow. We all

know and understand the need to be avenged and want God to deliver us from our "adversaries."

So what did Jesus say we needed to do to capture the attention of the Judge (God) and get results? He instructs us in language that is clear and to the point, so that we would realize this is what He is teaching us to do.

1. She came to him and presented her needs.

Jesus says we are to reach out to God, present ourselves to Him, and offer ourselves and our situation before Him, to show Him our resources (or lack of them), and our needs. We might find it difficult to be this specific, this detailed, this persistent, this blunt with God our Father, the Creator of the Universe. But Jesus instructs us to approach God in this way.

2. She continually came to bother him. She *"troubled"* him.

Jesus uses a word that implies the woman pushed the judge to the limits of his endurance, as far as he could go. She continued to bother him until he could not ignore her persistence. He had to listen and respond to her.

The Lord is teaching us this is the way we are to be with God. We are to continue to come into His Presence until He hears us, answers our prayers, and delivers us from our opponents.

3. She *"wearied"* him.

The word *"wearied"* describes the most intense kind of persistence. Jesus is saying we're to *weary* God the Father. We're to approach Him like a boxer who buffets the body of his opponent. Although this may sound sacrilegious to some, Jesus is indicating that we're to approach Him like we are *buffeting Him*. We're to be an "intolerable annoyance." We're to *"wear Him out."* (These are *Jesus'* words, not mine!)

When the woman did these three things, she received the results she needed from the judge. This is the model Jesus gives us for how we're to come before God!

4. Further, Jesus promised that God, Himself, would *"avenge His own elect who cry out day and night to Him."*

We're to raise a cry to God, speaking with a high, strong voice, imploring His help, expressing our needs, and being honest with Him, with our hearts filled with joy, pain, or any other condition of our mind, bodies, emotions, or spirits.

We all want God to answer our prayers speedily, to help us overcome our problems quickly, and to give us what we need as soon as possible. But does the Lord give us any clues for how we can receive instant answers? Yes!

Jesus said God avenges those of *"His own elect who cry out day and night to Him."* He answers *"speedily"* those who plead with Him persistently and continually. We need this kind of tenacity in our personal prayer lives.

We also need persistence in our prayers for our country. Persistent prayer brought about revival in Wales and Azusa Street. Persistent prayer is what brought about the revivals of Finney and Whitefield. It's what fueled the camp meetings that swept like wildfire through the West.

If we really want God to intervene in our nation, we must be people of persistent prayer. When we are, He will send revival and heal our land.

THE BLESSING OF BROKENNESS

One of the things that gets God attention is a broken and

contrite heart. When He sees brokenness from His people, He takes action. He responds.

There was a king of Israel named Hezekiah who was sick and about to die. He knew the importance of brokenness. The Bible says he turned his face to the wall (meaning he shut out every distraction). He got focused and intense. He prayed to the Lord and wept bitterly. God saw his brokenness and said, *"I've heard your prayer, I have seen your tears, I will heal you."* (2 Kings 20).

If we truly want God's attention, it's time for brokenness in our prayers and in our lives.

TAKE A LOOK IN THE MIRROR

For the Israelites, the Wilderness Tabernacle represented many things. It symbolized the place where God lived. It was a pattern to the people and to us today of how we are to approach God's Presence. It was also a model to them and to us of the kind of relationship the Father wants to have with His children. It was a place of sacrifice, offerings, repentance and forgiveness, a place of atonement and holiness, and a place where God spoke to His people.

One of the pieces of furniture God instructed Moses to build for the Tabernacle was a bronze laver. The laver was covered on the outside with the mirrors of the women who served at the doorway of the tent of meeting. They didn't have glass in those days, and so the most reflective surface they had was highly polished brass.

The women would continually polish these small pieces of brass until they became like a shinny mirror. These were the mirrors God instructed Moses to use in making the bronze laver, where the priests washed their hands and feet before they entered the Tabernacle (Exodus 30:18-21). It also was where the priests washed the actual sacrifices before they were offered on the altar.

The reason the bronze laver was covered with reflective mirrors was because God wanted the priests to be introspective, to examine themselves and see what was in their hearts and lives as they approached the very Presence of God.

Jesus was called the Light of the world. But did you know He also calls *us "the light of the world"* (Matthew 5:14)? That's right, as Christians we are to be lights that shine in the midst of the world's darkness.

Sadly, too many of us have let the world's darkness swallow up and hide our light. Instead of letting our light shine, we have allowed the world to become a bushel that covers our light.

It's time for us to take an introspective look in the mirror. Time to humble ourselves and ask God for forgiveness. Time to be the city set on a hill that Jesus has called us to be.

If we're going to see a return to righteousness in America, it must start with us, the Body of Christ. Unless we ourselves are righteous, how can we expect others to be?

If we truly want God's attention, it's time for brokenness in our prayers and in our lives.

So what can you do personally to bring righteousness back to America and stay the hand of God's judgment and destruction? Return to the Lord with your whole heart. Come before Him humbly, with a repentant, broken heart and ask for His forgiveness. Let's begin right now:

Father, as I pray for our country, I pray first for my own heart and life. Search me. Convict me of sin. Reveal if there is anything in my heart and life that displeases You. Forgive me. Cleanse me. Remove anything that separates me from You.

Thank You for all You have done for our nation. Thank You for the Pilgrims and those who came to this country to worship You. Thank You for the Founding Fathers who quoted from Your Word without embarrassment and gave us a country dedicated to freedom.

Father, our nation has gotten off track. We have disobeyed Your Word. We have tolerated sin and wickedness. We have allowed the ungodly to rule over us. Forgive us for sinning against You. Forgive us for ignoring and violating Your Word. Have mercy, I pray. Bring revival. Ignite my life with the fire of Your Spirit. Purge my life of sin, complacency, and compromise.

In Your name, I have authority over the work of the enemy in our nation. Satan, I bind you in Jesus' name. Be gone. You are defeated. Leave us alone. Take your hands off of God's people, His Church, my life, and this nation! Father God, may Your Spirit fall on our political, business, and military leaders. Remove all who deny Your sovereignty. Fill our government with leaders who declare You are their King.

May we be a people who first seek Your Kingdom and Your righteousness. May Your Spirit fall on our media. Bring about a revival in our television programs, films, Internet, music, and other media. Pour out Your Spirit on Hollywood.

Guide me in the decisions I make. Show me how to live for You. Bring revival to my life. To my church. To my family. To my community. To my neighborhood. Pour out Your Spirit. Give me boldness. Help me exercise the authority You have given me. I will not accept defeat, but instead, I declare victory in Your name. I love You, Lord. In Jesus' name. Amen.

Chapter Twenty-One

WHAT CAN YOU DO? PART 2

WHAT DOES THE WORLD SEE TODAY WHEN IT LOOKS at our country? How are we living as a people? More importantly, how are you living? To answer these questions, just consider the films, TV programs, and other "entertainment" we're exporting to the nations.

It can be easy to say, *"I'm* not producing immoral programs or movies. *I'm* not writing inappropriate books or composing ungodly music. It's not *my* fault." This may be true, but do your choices and decisions about what you do with your time and money contribute to the problem?

For the most part, the television industry lives or dies by ratings. If people aren't watching a particular program, it won't be long before it's yanked off the air. If a particular type of movie is made, and people don't go to the theater and buy a ticket to see it, producers and film studios will stop making those kinds of films. The same is true with books and music.

So what can *you* do? Stop watching the kind of programs on television that are dragging down our country, our society, and your spiritual life. Stop going to the kind of movies, listening to the kind of music, and reading the kind of books that tear you down instead of build you up.

When the television, movie, publication, and music industries start feeling the pressure in their wallets, they will get the message: This kind of garbage isn't what people want.

Every day, people make choices about what they'll do with their time, talent, and treasure. As Believers, we're called to be the light of the world. Light dispels darkness. It shows the way to go. It removes the fear of uncertainty. It's a powerful force…unless of course that light is hidden.

If your life were a book what kind of story would it tell? When people "read" who you vote for, how you spend your money, the kind of books you prefer, the television programs you watch, the movies you go to, the music you listen to, how you spend your money, what you do with your spare time, the kind of company you keep, and the habits you've developed in life…what story does your life tell?

My friend, your life is more than a book.

As Believers, we are citizens of *another* country. We're here to *colonize* this earth and make it a reflection of our King and His standards, His principles, and His righteousness.

We're here on this earth as His ambassadors to introduce and bring the Kingdom of Heaven to earth. So I ask you, do you stand out in this world or blend in? Do you have a voice for your King or have you been silenced? Is your light shining brightly, or has it grown dim?

A fierce battle is raging. Some might call it a cultural battle. Others consider it a war of ideas or moral standards. Some see it as a growing conflict between the East and the West. But this raging battle is so much more than these surface issues.

The *real* battle is in the spiritual realm. It's a battle for whose kingdom will reign on this earth. It's a battle over which kingdom we will declare our allegiance. Yes, it's a battle for the souls of men and women, boys and girls of every age, race, nationality, and color. But this war cannot be won unless you and I, and other Christians across this nation decide to get involved. You cannot wait for others to act.

You must decide to make a difference. "But what can *I* do?" I hear you asking.

Here are nine practical things you can do to take action:

1. Determine to which kingdom you will pledge your allegiance.

The Bible calls Believers *"aliens and strangers"* in the world (1 Peter 2:11). First John 2:15-17 tells us, this:

> *Do not love the world nor the things in the world. If anyone loves the world, the love of the Father is not in him. For all that is in the world, the lust of the flesh and the lust of the eyes and the boastful pride of life, is not from the Father, but is from the world. The world is passing away, and also its lusts; but the one who does the will of God lives forever.*

When Joshua and the children of Israel left Egypt and were on their way to the Promised Land, Joshua said,

> *Now, therefore, fear the LORD and serve Him in sincerity and truth; and put away the gods which your fathers served beyond the River and in Egypt, and serve the LORD. If it is disagreeable in your sight to serve the LORD, choose for yourselves today whom you will serve: whether the gods which your fathers served which were beyond the River, or the gods of the Amorites in whose land you are living; **but as for me and my house, we will serve the LORD** (Joshua 24:14-15).*

Jesus told us we are not of the world, but He has chosen us *out* of the world (John 15:19). He said He was not of (from) this world, and neither are we (John 17:14-16). You can't have dual citizenship. You're either a citizen of this world and part of its kingdom or your citizenship is of another world: Heaven.

2. Develop a discipline of reading the Bible every day.

The Bible is a light shining on our path and showing us the way to go. It is the "Owner's Manual" with instructions from our King about how we're to represent Him and His Kingdom on this earth.

Read it. Study it. Teach its principles to your children and grandchildren, and apply them in your daily behavior. Don't just *say* what you believe. Demonstrate your Kingdom citizenship by proving it through what you *do*.

3. Represent your King in public.

Be an example of Him in the places you go, the things you watch and listen to, the things you do. Support candidates who stand for what our King says is moral and right. Be ready to speak out on the issues. Write letters to the editor, attend public meetings, and even be willing to run for office yourself.

Don't be timid about your relationship with your King, but exercise your right to talk about God, the Church (His "called out ones"), and your beliefs (the Gospel message).

Don't hide your light under a bushel. Jesus said, *"Do not fear those who kill the body but are unable to kill the soul; but rather fear Him who is able to destroy both soul and body in hell"* (Matthew 10:28).

In this world, others may be able to harm you in some short-term way, but God wants you to be more concerned about pleasing Him.

4. Take political issues seriously.

Make sure you are registered to vote and that you *do* vote. Then encourage others to go to the polls. Study the issues and learn the different positions that politicians have on them. Have an informed opinion.

We have a duty and an obligation to stand for righteousness in everything we do. This includes politics. When we vote, we need to remember we have a primary allegiance and responsibility to God and His Kingdom. This means we need to elect people who will take a stand for our King and His righteousness.

If both candidates profess allegiance to the Almighty, we need to consider who demonstrates it the most. The sobering reality is that many candidates will say anything to get elected. We need to look at their "fruit" and recognize that actions truly do speak louder than words. True convictions are born out in actions.

We have a duty and an obligation to stand for righteousness in everything we do.

Some candidates have tried to masquerade as Christians. They have talked about growing up in the Church and the importance of moral principles. Some even quote from the Bible or the teachings of Jesus. Others have paid lip service to Believers, talking about subjects they have studied, good deeds they have done, and people who have influenced them.

But the Bible has given us one crucial test: Who is their King? Who is their Lord?

If Jesus is their Lord, they will state this clearly, and they will act accordingly. Support such men and women!

5. Be an example of our King and His standards in your own home and with your family.

Too many Believers today have allowed their lives to be filled with compromise. They have been corrupted by the world, particularly through the images and thoughts spread by the media.

Be sure you remember what the Bible says concerning compromise. Make a personal commitment to righteousness.

Be like Job and make a covenant with your eyes (Job 31:1). Say with David, *"I will set no worthless thing before my eyes"* (Psalm 101:3). Vow not to allow your vision to be clouded with anything that displeases God or allows sin to enter your life or your home.

Instead, think on those things that are good, true, honorable, right, pure, beautiful, and worthy of praise (Philippians 4:8). Be certain you have made the Word of God the standard for your life.

Make a commitment to keep your home clean and pure. Eliminate anything that is worthless and not virtuous or that might tempt you to abandon Biblical standards. Insist on Scriptural principles for the things you and your family see, read, and hear.

6. Guard your "gates"!

Remember the influence the media can have on you and your family.

There's nothing more powerful on earth than a simple thought. Ideas and what we think about control the world. Thoughts are so powerful that people attend universities and pay thousands of dollars to read and study the concepts and conclusions of people who have long since left this earth.

Solomon said, *"As a man thinks in his heart, so is he"* (Proverbs 23:7). The literal translation is "as he thinks in his subconscious mind." (This verse isn't referring to an anatomical organ of the body!) How do thoughts get into your heart? By what we allow to enter through two of our five "gates."

We have five natural senses – five "gateways" – into our body, soul, and spirit. Our eyes and ears are two vital entrances. By seeing and hearing things often enough or long enough, these sights and sounds begin to form thoughts in our mind. What we are continually exposed to eventually will enter our heart – and it's out of our heart that we will live.

If people are what they think in their hearts, and if someone wants to "control" or "influence" them, their thought life has to be controlled and influenced.

Whoever, or whatever, governs the thoughts of a nation, provides the principles by which that nation lives. This is why the battle for man is really a struggle for his heart.

We influence people's hearts and their subconscious minds through pictures, images, sights, sounds, words, and music. Ephesians 2:1-3 says God made us alive who were *"dead in [our] trespasses and sins, in which we formerly walked according to the course of this world, according to the prince of the power of the air, of the spirit who is now working in the sons of disobedience."*

As I stated earlier, Paul reminds us in Ephesians 6:12 that we don't wrestle against flesh and blood...but against the rulers of the darkness of this age, against spiritual hosts of wickedness in the atmosphere.

Therefore, people's behavior, values, beliefs, relationships with God, and their very thoughts are the result of the influence of a spirit who is the *"prince of the power of the air."*

The air has waves...radio waves...television waves...sound waves...light waves...voice and data transmissions, and satellite signals. So when we turn on the radio or television, go to a movie, or connect to the Internet, we're connecting to the "waves" in the "air."

These words, sounds, and pictures enter through our gateways and make their way into our "hearts" over and over again.

This is why Satan wants to control the media and why he wants to rule it with perversity. Whoever can govern the air...the waves...sounds...pictures...and light...can rule the hearts and minds of people. It's the power of the air.

Ask God to help you monitor and control what you allow in your home and in your own life. Just as King David said in Psalm 101 that he wouldn't set anything wicked or evil in front of his eyes, this is an essential Covenant for us to make with our own eyes today.

7. Encourage others to take a stand for righteousness.

Can you imagine what would happen if by the millions, God's people – citizens of Heaven living here on this earth – made a commitment to stand and speak up for what their King says and what they believe? What would happen if Christians would begin to pray, repent before the Lord, and ask His forgiveness for *our* many transgressions?

What would happen if we all would begin to intercede for our nation and the world?

Encourage your friends, family members, neighbors, and people in your church to read this message and take action.

Don't wait for someone else to lead the commitment to righteousness! The prophet said, *"Sow with a view to righteousness, reap in accordance with kindness; break up your fallow ground, for it is time to seek the LORD"* (Hosea 10:12). God is looking for people like this...looking for people like *you*...who will Sow Seeds of right living.

8. Support ministries, churches, and people who truly take a stand for righteousness.

Give to ministries dedicated to making the kingdoms of this earth the Kingdom of our Lord and King. Support ministries who are declaring spiritual war on the enemy and committed to seeing this great nation of America return to the Christian foundations upon which it was established and built.

Make it a priority to partner with ministries like ours that are on the front lines. Pray for us and others who are committed to God's Kingdom. And support them with your prayers, finances, and encouragement.

9. Make a serious commitment to prayer.

In a letter dated March 14, 1493, written from Lisbon, Portugal, Christopher Columbus wrote, "God is wont to hear the prayers of His servants who love His precepts even to the performance of apparent impossibilities." To Columbus, the discovery of the New World had been a miracle. And throughout his life, he realized that God answered prayer.[108]

Today, America needs another miracle. We need a powerful visitation from God.

The fate of America – and the world – is in our hands. But we can't expect God to bring about change unless His people make a commitment to pray.

Will *you* pray? Will you pray violently (Matthew 11:12)? Will you continually and persistently seek the Father?

People everywhere are telling us that Jesus and belief in Him is not relevant. Best-selling books contend that God could not possibly exist. Television programs and movies ridicule those who believe in Him. Skeptics tell us we are foolish to trust in a Higher Power who is the One, True God

But remember that people also were saying similar things before the great revivals that shook America as God sovereignly moved over them. He demonstrated in miraculous ways that He was real and that His power and Kingdom has no end.

In these pages, I've shown how often God moved in answer to the prayers of average men and women. There was nothing extraordinary about Evan Roberts, Jeremiah Lanphier, or Frank Bartleman. Great outpourings of the Spirit were the result of the prayers of individuals whose names we don't even know.

They didn't wait for a movement to start or for a formal invitation to intercede. Rather, men and women simply dedicated themselves to prayer. They were committed never to stop calling on God until He heard their prayers and sent revival.

Don't wait for God to raise up someone else. Devote yourself to prayer, and lead by example. Start praying! And don't just pray polite prayer. Pray intensely. Seek God. And put your faith into action.

Chapter Twenty-Two

MY PRAYER FOR YOU AND AMERICA

GOD HAS GIVEN AMERICA A CHOICE. IT IS A decision that begins with each person. It starts with me. And it starts with you.

My prayer is that we wake up, repent, and return to righteousness. We can avoid or postpone the need for God to pour out His judgment...**IF** all of us from the poor house to the White House make this decision!

We need a mighty revival and a return to righteousness among churches and church leaders. We must recognize that we face a crisis.

As a nation and as individuals, we have fallen so far away from God's standards of righteousness that I sometimes wonder if we've passed the point of no return. I ask myself, "Are we on the Eve of Destruction? Have we angered God so much that He is getting ready to pour out His wrath and His judgment? He said that He Himself would show the world that He is the one true God."

How many years, months, or even days do we have to turn things around? Personally, I think we are running out of time. But the Bible makes it clear: God can change His mind and be merciful...*if* we repent and return to righteousness.

Moses intervened when God was about to destroy Israel, and the Lord *"changed His mind"* (Exodus 32:14). When David sinned against the people, his offering and sacrifice stayed the hand of the angel God had sent to destroy Jerusalem (2 Samuel 24:16).

Has the Almighty made up His mind to send judgment to America and the world? If so, might He change His mind? I believe anything is possible if we repent.

But we need to face the fact that, as a nation, we have sinned. Many people today don't want to discuss the concept of sin and iniquity. They don't like to be told what to do or how to live – and they certainly don't want to hear about the consequences of living contrary to God's Word. They ignore that the Bible says the wages of sin are death (Romans 6:23). We need to return to God. Unless we do, our freedoms will continue to be eroded.

WHAT WILL IT TAKE?

America drew Japan to its knees with two atomic bombs. After the first, there may have been questions. When the second one dropped, they hoisted the white flag.

We've seen the impact of the 9-11 terrorist attacks. Is this the end of such terrible devastation or just the beginning? Our adversaries are ruthless and determined. But they also want us to be afraid and weak. They will not give up.

What is it going to take for us to change our ways?

Today, nations like Iran have clearly stated they are intent on developing nuclear weapons (if they haven't already) and that they intend to share their bombs with every Islamic state. They are determined to find a way to bring our nation under its domination. Their ultimate goal is for America, Israel, the West, and all Christians and Jews to submit or die.

How many dirty bombs will it take exploding in our cities before we're ready to wave the white flag? How long before Islam brings America to its knees? How long before we say, "We surrender"? Or should that tragedy ever happen, will we be strong enough to take immediate, decisive, and forceful action? The only thing radical Islamists respect is force. Inaction is interpreted as weakness.

What happens if hate-filled Islamists find a way to build and detonate an electromagnetic bomb over the U.S.? We would return to the dark ages!

Some think we shouldn't even consider such possibilities. But who could have imagined that a 9-11 could take place? As unthinkable as this was in the past, so many don't want to consider what might occur tomorrow.

I believe God wants us to take this issue seriously. Very seriously. We need to ask ourselves, "What is the price of freedom? How many of our liberties are we willing to relinquish to remain a free people? What are we willing to do for this privilege? How much are we really willing to pay for freedom?"

THE POWER TO CHANGE

Our only hope is in God. This is why we must return to His Kingdom and submit to the Lordship of Jesus Christ. We need to live according to His principles. If we don't, we are doomed to suffer the consequences. We are headed in a direction that cannot bring anything but destruction, unless there is repentance.

In 1831, Alexis de Tocqueville looked at our country and saw that we stood for righteousness and our Christian faith. What does the world see when they view us today?

Many see our commitment to Christianity through our dedication to missions and evangelism. Some see our generous heart through the outpouring of relief efforts during famines and disasters. But others look at the heart of America through our exportation of entertainment. This has been called "cultural imperialism," as many throughout the world resent the kind of lifestyle we are promoting. To what are they referring? Not Christianity. Not compassion or benevolence.

They are talking about the American dominance of the entertainment business. They are speaking of the violence, godlessness, and filth that characterize so many of our films and television programs.

Our culture's obsession with sex, inhumanity, and immorality is one of the primary reasons Muslims hate our nation so much.

But we have the power to change all of this. We don't have to wait for Hollywood to take the first step. Change can start with each of us. *Right now.*

I'm referring to living your life according to God's Word. Be a watchman over what you allow in your heart and mind, and do not tolerate any form of ungodliness in your home or life. Be dedicated to prayer...violent prayer. Intense prayer. Selfless prayer. Vigilant prayer.

I am talking about letting your light shine, putting your faith into action, and fulfilling your responsibilities as a Believer – voting and supporting candidates who stand for righteousness and Christian principles.

THE KEY TO RESTORATION

The Almighty spoke through the prophets of old, who realized that Israel needed to return to Him. In fact, in the fourth chapter of Amos *alone,* God warned the people *five times* why they needed to change, but He concluded, *"Yet you have not returned to Me."*

In the time of Hosea, this righteous man realized God's people had sinned. They had lost their "first love." Their lives had become consumed with immorality and wickedness. Even though God still loved them, He had no choice but to send judgment. They had to experience the serious consequences of their actions. But God's judgment was not the last word. Even after sending His wrath, the Lord still deeply cared and wanted them to enjoy the full benefits of His Kingdom. He still desired to bless them in every way.

> **Our culture's obsession with sex, inhumanity, and immorality is one of the primary reasons Muslims hate our nation so much.**

So, Hosea cried out to the people, *"Come, let us return to the LORD. For He has torn us, but He will heal us; He has wounded us, but He will bandage us"* (Hosea 6:1).

The children of Israel were a people in need of healing and restoration. God was ready to respond, but first they needed to return to Him. They needed to take action. The people could not continue to live in sin, lead an immoral lifestyle, and behave in ways that violated His Word. They needed to repent, confess, and make changes in their conduct.

These important principles from Amos and Hosea apply to America today. God does not desire to judge us, but, as He did with Israel, He has no choice if we choose to disobey Him and violate His Word.

May God help us to search our hearts to see if we have drifted away from Him. If we have fallen in love with the world and allowed our love for Him to grow cold. If He no longer has first place in our lives. If we are serving other gods. If our hearts are filled with pride, if we are seeking our own kingdom rather than His.

May we return to Him, repent of our sins, and seek Him anew and afresh. He is waiting to restore us, heal us, and enable us to experience His bountiful blessings.

Our only hope as a nation is to turn back to God. To cry out to Him, to rekindle our faith, and to put that faith into action in our lives.

Don't be one of those Christians who sits back and does nothing. Don't wait for others to take the lead. *You* have the power to make a difference and help bring this nation back to God, back to righteousness. Vote. Get involved. Pray. And be bold in everything you do.

Remember: You are a child of the King. You are a citizen of His Kingdom. He has given you delegated authority. Use it today!

Chapter Twenty-Three

WHAT THIS MEANS TO YOU

ON THE MORNING OF SEPTEMBER 11, 2001, ALMOST 3,000 people went to work thinking they would return home at the end of the day. But they didn't.

The thought of death and the possibility of no longer seeing loved ones certainly cause people to think about spending more time with their families. We've all probably heard it said, "When you're on your death bed, the last thing you're wishing is that you had spent more time on your job."

I'm told that every day, near the top of the President's agenda is a "Threat Assessment Briefing." This is because the threats are real. The strong sense out of Washington is not "if" terrorist organizations will strike again, but *where, when,* and *how hard* will the next attack occur.

All of us need to reflect on what's next for America. But right now I want you to think about what's next for *you!*

There are two kinds of people reading this book. Some have a personal relationship with Jesus Christ. And some don't.

If you are one of those who doesn't know Jesus, perhaps you are one of the many who since September 11 began searching for a meaningful relationship with God. Possibly you feel a vacuum, an emptiness in your life you can't explain. Perhaps you feel something is missing. Maybe you've tried many things to fill that void.

If so, you're not alone. There's a God-shaped vacuum inside everyone. Something within us drives us to seek ultimate meaning. That "something" is placed there by the Creator. You were made to have fellowship with God, and your inner man desperately wants to know Him.

That emptiness inside you, inside each of us, can only be filled when we come into right relationship with the Father through His Son, Jesus Christ.

The Bible tells us our sins have separated us from God. That's why He sent His Son to this world: to pay the penalty for your sins and mine.

You can know God deeply and personally, and in doing so, you can experience His awesome power in your life.

God is not interested in your works. Your noble deeds won't save you. He wants you to trust Him and accept His free gift of salvation.

Many people think their ticket to Heaven is being good, so they spend their lives trying to be worthy enough to go there when they die. Wrong! No one can ever be good enough or earn their way into Heaven.

God is not waiting for you to do "good" or get "cleaned up" before He will save you or accept you. He says, "I'll receive you just the way you are…and then I will help you transform your life."

What do you have to do to experience salvation? It's simple. The Bible, clearly states, *"Believe in the Lord Jesus Christ and you will be saved"* (Acts 16:31).

God's Word also says that whoever calls on the name of the Lord will be saved (Romans 10:13). It's so easy...just call on Him. When was the last time you called on God? Perhaps now is the time.

BUILDING ON THE ROCK

The Bible tells the story of two men who each built a house. One constructed his dwelling on solid rock, the other on sand.

When the storms arrived, when the rain fell and the wind blew, the house of the man that was built on the rock stood firm against the elements. But the house of the man that was built on sand...it fell and was destroyed (Matthew 7:24-29). Jesus tells us this story to help us think about the undergirding of our lives and to help us realize we need a strong foundation...or we are vulnerable, just as so many people were on September 11, 2001.

Today, what is your foundation made of?

A man serving in our Armed Forces recently said on one of our television programs, "Peace only accepts one kind of payment, and that's blood . . ."

He was right in the natural world – and he was right in the spiritual world.

Peace does require payment. Jesus Christ paid what was due for you and me. He loves you...cares about you...and wants to be the solid rock upon which you build your life.

It's because of the Cross and the empty tomb that you don't have to be afraid or worry, "What could happen to me?" or "What will happen next?"

It's possible for you to know God deeply and intimately. It isn't enough just to believe Jesus was a good man. You have to confess Him as Lord, ask Him to forgive your sins, and receive Him into your heart as Savior.

To my Christian friends reading this book, *September 11th should have been a wake-up call to all of us and to America.*

It's sad to say, but while our nation was clearly *shaken* by the events of September 11, 2001, the devastation doesn't seem to have brought about much lasting change, at least not spiritually.

What will it take for us to wake up and return to righteousness?

In this book I've tried to make it historically clear that ours is a nation founded by God-fearing leaders, most of whom were Christians. We are a people whose laws were based on the Bible, a country that has been blessed by God. A nation whose money is inscribed with the words, "In God We Trust." But we are far from God. Our Pledge of Allegiance has even been declared unconstitutional because of the words, "One nation, under GOD…"

At a time when we should be humbling ourselves, seeking the Lord, repenting, and calling on Him for mercy, many Americans are crying out in their own way, *"We do not want this man* [Jesus Christ] *to reign over us!"* (Luke 19:14)

What will it take for us to wake up and return to righteousness?

Have we totally grasped who the REAL enemy is? Yes, we know who the PEOPLE behind it are. But as Christians, are we hesitant to acknowledge this is really a SPIRITUAL WAR?

Yes, radical, extremist Muslims are at the forefront of terrorist activity throughout the world. But in reality, they are the "symptom," not the "cause." They are what we see on the *surface* in the *natural world* but not what is at the *root* in the *spiritual world*.

THIS IS A SPIRITUAL WAR!

The book of Ephesians tells us that we do not wrestle against flesh and blood, but against principalities, against powers, against the rulers of the darkness of this age, against spiritual hosts of wickedness in the heavenly places (Ephesians 6:12).

2 Corinthians 10:3-6 reminds us,

For though we live in the world, we do not wage war as the world does. The weapons we fight with are not the weapons of the world. On the contrary, they have divine power to demolish strongholds. We demolish arguments and every pretension that sets itself up against the knowledge of God, and we take captive every thought to make it obedient to Christ.

There is a battle raging between God and Satan. There is a spiritual war being fought between those who are true followers of Christ and those who follow false gods and the devil, who has them terribly deceived.

As Christians, we're supposed to know the truth:

* ✴ We are supposed to know about spiritual warfare.

* ✴ We are supposed to be aware of End-Time prophecy and have discernment for spiritual things.

* ✴ We are supposed to be spiritual watchmen, standing guard against the attacks of the enemy, ready in a moment to blow the trumpet and sound the alarm.

Part of the problem is that many Christians today have been seduced by the devil and by the world's systems. Afraid of what other people might think or say. Too caught up in the "things" we have to do, worry about, or think about, to take the time to heed the words of 2 Chronicles 7:14, which need repeating until they penetrate our very soul:

*If **my people**, which are called by **my name**, will humble themselves, pray, seek my face, **turn from their wicked ways**, **THEN** I will hear from heaven, and will forgive their sin, and will heal their land.*

WHAT WILL YOU DO?

My friend, it's time we fasted, prayed and sought God's face. It is time we humbled ourselves before Him, repented, and cried out to Him for revival in our nation and the world. If we, as the Church of the living God, aren't doing this, who will?

We are a blessed people! We enjoy so many freedoms. But we stand to lose much of our blessing and quite possibly, freedom itself, if we don't open our eyes to what is happening around us and take action!

In his "Thanksgiving Day Proclamation" in 1863, President Abraham Lincoln said,

We have been the recipients of the choicest bounties of heaven. We have been preserved these many years in peace and prosperity. We have grown in numbers, wealth and power, as no nation has ever grown. But we have forgotten God. It behooves us, then, to humble ourselves before the Offended Power, to confess our national sins, and to pray for clemency and forgiveness.

It's time that we as the Body of Christ raise a righteous standard. It's time for us to stand in the gap, grab hold of the horns of the altar, and cry out to God for forgiveness and mercy. We must shake off the seduction of the world that has tried to put us in chains. Now is the hour for us to wage real spiritual warfare.

As I wrote in Chapter 20, Jesus tells us the Kingdom of Heaven suffers violence, and violent people take it by force (Matthew 11:12). We have to get *spiritually violent!* Not in the form of protests, marches, boycotts, or anything else in the natural world. We've got to get violent in the spiritual world! It's time to tear down the strongholds of the enemy, to bind the powers of darkness, and to loose the powers of light and righteousness.

Remember, God said *only* when we humble ourselves, turn from our wicked ways, and seek His face would He forgive our sin and heal our land.

Our nation needs to be healed. Will you be a part of the healing process?

Are you ready to get serious about praying for our country and the world? The Bible says that one can put a thousand to flight and two can put ten thousand to flight (Deuteronomy 32:30). May we join our faith and prayers together and bombard the heavens, asking God for spiritual restoration.

Let's pray for America. Pray for our leaders. Pray for those in government and in authority. Pray for safety and protection over our beloved land. Pray for revival.

Studies also say almost 49% of Christians go to churches where the pastor doesn't have a true Biblical worldview.

Chapter Twenty-Four

AMERICA
AT THE
CROSSROADS

THIS IS A BOOK ABOUT AMERICA. ITS PAST AND ITS future. But also its present. Just look around today. What do you see?

You'll find that America is a divided nation. We're separated – not just by liberal and conservative viewpoints – but we're divided by standards of righteousness and morality.

My friend, there are only two powers in the entire world, and I'm not speaking of Republican or Democratic, conservative or liberal. I'm talking about the forces of good and evil, God and Satan, and the greatest power on earth is not political, economic, or military. It is the power of Almighty God.

Many would like to erase God from our society and go their own selfish way. They profess they are interested in diversity, but they're really talking about pluralism. These two philosophies aren't the same. Diversity acknowledges there are a number of opinions, but pluralism says that, since there are so many opinions, no one belief system can claim to be right.

The fact is simply this: One way *is* right. There is a God in Heaven. Not *many* gods but **one** God. He's the God of the Bible. And there is a very real and literal devil.

Both God and Satan have a plan for your life and for America. The Father's plan is to bless and prosper us, to give us hope and a future. Satan's scheme is to kill, steal, and destroy us individually and as a nation.

So we have a choice to make about which plan we will follow and who we will serve. The Bible tells us, *"Righteousness exalts a nation: but sin is a reproach to any people"* (Proverbs 14:34). When we are serving God and exalting a righteous standard, He blesses us. When we fall into sin and immorality, and turn from serving Him and the principles of His Word, our sin brings a reproach and the hand of God's blessing is removed from us.

There are consequences to the choices we make in life, for good or for bad.

Our Heavenly Father wants us to live according to the precepts of His Word. He longs to have a personal relationship with us. He desires for us to serve Him, love Him, and obey Him. We sense His heart when He said, *"You shall love the Lord your God with all your heart, with all your soul, with all your might"* (Deuteronomy 6:5). We are also told, *"Love the Lord your God, and keep His charge, and His statutes, and His judgments, and His commandments, always"* (Deuteronomy 11:1).

There are consequences to the choices we make in life, for good or for bad. God promises positive outcomes if we hear and obey Him. He says, *"If you listen carefully to My commandments, if you'll love Me, if you'll serve Me with all your heart, with all your soul, I will bless you."*

But God also warns us to *"take heed to yourselves, that your heart be not deceived, and that you turn not aside and serve other gods, and worship them"* (Deuteronomy 11:16 KJV). He cautions if we do, He will be forced to send His wrath against us, and we will reap the consequences of our actions.

God sets choices before you and me. Listen to what He told the children of Israel:

> *I set before you this day a blessing and a curse; a bless-ing, if you obey the commandments of the Lord your God, which I command you this day; and a curse, if you will not obey the commandments of the Lord your God, but turn aside out of the way which I command you this day, to go after other gods, which you have not known* (Deuteronomy 11:26-28).

TRUTH NEVER CHANGES

A majority of people in this country call themselves Christians. Yet millions of Believers don't read the Bible, and countless of those who say they read it don't know basic Bible truths. And far too many live by their preferences rather than by Biblical principles. Studies also say almost 49% of Christians go to churches where the pastor doesn't have a true Biblical worldview. This means he doesn't believe the Bible is the inspired Word of God. He doesn't, in many cases, even believe Jesus rose from the dead.

Is it any wonder God's people are confused and don't know what to believe or how to live?

Sadly, many deny the principle of "absolute truth." Still others question, "What are the absolutes?" One thing is for certain, we can't allow the points on our compass to turn with the wind, or we will never know which direction we're headed.

As the Bible warns us, many have chosen to turn aside from following God's commandments. We've sought after other gods. We have followed the god of immorality. We've worshiped the idols of promiscuity, pornography, materialism, political correctness, tolerance, and inclusiveness of sin.

And we have embraced relativism, which says everything's right sometime, and nothing is right every time. We have worshiped the idol of "feel-good living." If it feels good, do it!

Our nation's standard for morality has disintegrated to the point where anything sexual is morally acceptable as long as it takes place between consenting adults.

But regardless of what some people want to believe, there really *are* absolute truths, and these truths apply to all people at all times, regardless of their faith or lack of faith, and regardless of the situation. These absolutes are found in the Word of God.

One of those unalterable truths is that there is only one way to Heaven. Jesus said, *"I am the way, the truth, and the life: no man comes to the Father, but by me"* (John 14:6). Christianity claims that salvation is received as a gift from God. Other faiths claim redemption is earned through good deeds. Both can't be right. Absolute truth, by definition, rejects other claims of truth.

There are those in America who would agree with our right to believe this for ourselves…just as long as we don't try to convince them to believe it too. For them, to claim that Jesus' words apply to everyone is to be "intolerant." Some would even go so far as to call it "hate speech" when we call sin a "sin."

We have judges today who apparently believe the First Amendment, which guarantees freedom of speech and worship, applies to everyone except Christians who want to pray in Jesus' Name.

Many in America have turned aside from following the commandments of the Lord. We've chosen personal preference over God's principles.

SALT AND LIGHT

I believe God is calling us as a people and as a nation to return to Him in righteousness. The Bible tells us, *"The fear of the LORD is to hate evil; pride and arrogance and the evil way"* (Proverbs 8:13). Yes, we are supposed to *despise* evil, not tolerate it. This doesn't mean to hate the person who's committing evil; rather we're supposed to hate the sin itself.

Someone once said, "Change comes about because of passion or persecution." I pray we choose passion over persecution in this country. I pray God doesn't have to pour out His judgment on us, America, or on the Church before we take responsibility and really become salt and light in this nation (Matthew 5:13-16).

Scripture says, *"You are the children of the Lord your God: you are a holy people to the Lord your God, and the Lord has chosen you to be a peculiar people to himself, above all the nations that are on the earth"* (Deuteronomy 14:1-2). Clearly, we have a decision to make.

And we have choices to make regarding how we live. Remember, the Bible states,

> *I have set before you life and death, blessing and cursing: therefore choose life that both you and your seed may live. That you would love the Lord your God, and that you would obey his voice, and that you would cleave to him: for he is your life, and the length of your days* (Deuteronomy 30:19-20).

Friend, we must decide. It's time for us as the true, Blood-bought, redeemed Church of the living God to...

* Acknowledge our personal sins
* Repent in humility before God

*Repent for the sins of our nation

*Stand up for what we believe

*Put on the whole armor of God

*Wage spiritual warfare

*Storm the gates of hell

*Speak up

*Be salt and light in this generation

*Call America back to repentance and righteousness!

God is weary of our meaningless words. Isaiah 29:13 says, *"This people draw near with their words and honor Me with their lip service, but they remove their hearts far from Me."*

The Bible encourages us to *"Seek the Lord while He may be found; to call on Him while He's near, to let the wicked forsake his way and the unrighteous man his thoughts; and let him return to the Lord."* We are promised that, if we do, *"God will have compassion on him, God will abundantly pardon"* (Isaiah 55:6-7).

The prophet Joel warned us that *"the day of the Lord is indeed great and very awesome, and; who can endure it?"* he asked.

"Yet even now," declares the Lord, *"Return to Me with all your heart, and with fasting, weeping and mourning; and rend your heart and not your garments. Now return to the* Lord *your God, for He is gracious and compassionate, slow to anger, abounding in lovingkindness and relenting of evil"* (Joel 2:11-13).

The Church must lead America in a return to righteous living. The Bible warns us,

For the time is come that judgment must begin at the house of God: and if it first begins at us, what shall the end be of them that obey not the gospel of God? And if the

righteous scarcely be saved, where shall the ungodly and the sinner appear? (1 Peter 4:17-18).

God is saying to us, "Humble yourselves, repent, seek My face, and turn from your wicked ways" (2 Chronicles 7:14). He's asking us to take a stand for righteousness in this nation, not just with lip service but with our deeds. He wants us to remember that we're not fighting against flesh and blood, but against principalities, against powers, against the rulers of the darkness of this world, against what the Bible calls *"spiritual wickedness in high places"* (Ephesians 6:12 KJV).

God wants us to know that the weapons of our warfare are not carnal but mighty to the pulling down of strongholds. He wants us to remember that though we walk in the flesh, we do not war after the flesh (2 Corinthians 10:3-4).

The hour has come for the Church to storm the gates of hell!

In every political administration, we must continue to diligently pray for our President, Cabinet, and all elected leaders in America as the Bible compels us to in 1 Timothy 2:1-3. We must keep our nation and the peace of Jerusalem always at the forefront of our prayers and efforts (Psalm 122:5-7).

We need to pray that those who govern us will make decisions which uphold Biblical principles and take a stand for righteousness. As the Body of Christ, we must lead this country by our example. I urge you to pray for every elected official on Capitol Hill, whether they're Democrat or Republican, that their decisions would be guided by God Almighty.

WE ARE STEWARDS

We have a responsibility under God for our nation. The Apostle Paul said, *"It's required of stewards that one be found trustworthy"* (1 Corinthians 4:2). Each of us as individuals, and all of us together, are stewards of our great country. If Believers choose to abandon our stewardship of America, what will we say when God judges this land?

Earlier, I talked about the parable of the talents. The Bible records how the man who did nothing with his talent was cast into outer darkness, *"where there will be weeping and gnashing of teeth"* (Matthew 29:30). We have a responsibility to take specific action... or we will be judged accordingly!

I believe we have an obligation to live and act based on the Truth of God's Word and not according to our own selfish desires. Let me be blunt. The Lord isn't a Republican or a Democrat, an Independent or a Libertarian. But I have what may be news for you. He *is* a monarchist. And He is just what the Bible calls Him: *"The King of Kings and Lord of Lords"* (Revelation 19:16)!

* The Bible says, *"At the name of Jesus, every knee will bow, of those who are in heaven and on earth and under the earth, and that every tongue will confess that Jesus Christ is Lord, to the glory of God the Father"* (Philippians 2:10-11).

* Scripture tells us, *"The kingdoms of this world has become the kingdom of our Lord and of His Christ; and He will reign forever and ever"* (Revelation 11:15).

* Jesus prayed to the Father, *"Thy kingdom come, Thy will be done, on earth as it is in heaven"* (Matthew 6:10 KJV).

* The Bible declares, *"the earth is the Lord's"* (Psalms 24:1). That's right. The earth is **God's Kingdom.**

WHAT IS YOUR POSITION?

The Lord has given us a free will and the power to choose, but He wants our choices to be based on the truth of His Word and His righteousness, not on the perceived truth of man. So when you are asked, "What's your position on abortion?" or "What is your opinion on homosexuality or same sex marriages?" your answer should be, "Here's what my King says."

The Church has been in a dangerous sleep for too many years. While apathy has crept into our hearts, we've seen many of our freedoms diminish. The great Christian writer, G. K. Chesterton said, "Once you abolish God, the government becomes god." And we're living out his words today.

> I believe we have an obligation to live and act based on the Truth of God's Word and not according to our own selfish desires.

Our government now preaches its own philosophy to our children. Not God's. For example, it's against the law for a 12-year-old girl to drive an automobile. It's illegal for her to drink alcohol, yet state governments will sponsor the distribution of birth control pills to her at this young age, and in some states, the authorities will assist her in obtaining an abortion without even telling her parents. The government, as god, is saying, "We won't let you drive. We won't let you smoke. We won't even let you take an aspirin in school without a note from your parents, but we will help you be sexually promiscuous, and we'll help *eliminate* any children you might have if you become pregnant."

And while the government is openly promoting the permissiveness of sexual promiscuity through our schools, it also is now teaching our children that homosexual marriage and homosexual sex is normal and acceptable.

The government, as "god," says you can't legislate morality, but think about it! All legislation is driven by morals. You and I may disagree on exactly what they are, but morals are the basis of all law and every legal code that's ever been written or signed.

WHAT WILL YOU SAY?

Christians are rightly concerned about the erosion of liberties. We see the Ten Commandments stripped from the walls of our courts. We see prayer in school criminalized like drugs. We see sexual immorality and abomination praised as an alternative lifestyle and promoted by our tax dollars and the entertainment industry, but none of these wrongs excuse us from hiding in the sanctuary and ignoring our responsibility to take a stand for righteousness. We say it's wonderful to live in a free country, but I ask you today, what difference does it make?

> **America is truly at a crossroads. Political correctness rules the day. We're encouraged to be tolerant and inclusive rather than live by Biblical principles.**

It's true, they have removed the Ten Commandments from some of our courtrooms, but when was the last time you sat down to read them to your children or for your own benefit? Prayer in school has been outlawed, but do you have a family prayer time with your children at home? Will you live and die as a free citizen, yet never once act on your right to petition government by writing a letter to your congressman or senator?

You say, "Well, David, what difference will my letter make?" Well, on that day when God judges America, I ask you, what will we say?

* We who have been given by God the power of personal liberty and freedom, what will we have done with it?

* We who have been given the freedom of speech, what will we have said?

* We who have been given the freedom to publish, what will we have written?

* The freedom to travel. Where will we have gone?

* The freedom to worship. When and how will we have worshiped?

* The freedom to vote. Did we cast our vote according to God's laws?

Yes, America is a great nation, and it was birthed by brave men and women who put their faith above their desire for wealth and prestige. Our national anthem ends in a question:

"Oh, say does that star-spangled banner yet wave
O'er the land of the free and the home of the brave?"

This isn't just the prelude to a baseball game. It's a question we've asked ourselves for 200 years and one this generation must ask and respond to as well. Are we, as Christians, brave enough to stand up to the tyranny of secular humanism and do our part?

Friend, its time Believers in America stopped being the passive, silent majority. We must ask forgiveness for ourselves and for our nation, and ask the Lord to send a mighty revival to our land. We need God's promise of healing and forgiveness to be made alive in our day. If not, we're going to stay anchored to our church pew and forget that faith without works is dead.

THE RIGHT PATH

America is truly at a crossroads. Political correctness rules the day. We're encouraged to be tolerant and inclusive rather than live by Biblical principles. We've allowed America to almost become a post-Christian society. The moral fabric of our nation, the foundation, has disintegrated.

Millions of Christians have become numb to the darkness that's invaded our homes and families. What society once considered morally unacceptable is now broadcast on television every night in prime time. What the Bible calls "sin" is now viewed as an "alternative lifestyle," and when you and I try to uphold Biblical values, we're labeled intolerant. While today's media calls for tolerance, they censor righteousness and morality.

We live in a world of situational ethics. For too many, truth has become subjective. Society encourages people to define truth for themselves according to their own desires. Again, "If it feels good, do it." Untold millions believe if they go to church, if they are a good person, then that makes them a Christian. Others believe finding God, if there is one, is like traveling to Chicago. You can get there by plane, train, or automobile. It doesn't matter what path you take or what religion you follow as long as you arrive at the destination.

YOUR VOICE MATTERS

Yes, America is facing a time of decision. The spirit of the antichrist is more prevalent today than at any time in our spiritual history. This spirit, which wars against Christ and Christianity, is doing everything possible to undermine, deny, and reject the truth of God's Son.

The Bible warns that apostasy (or a falling away) will come to the Church before the return of our Lord and that once people abandon the faith, they will follow deceiving spirits. They will be lovers of themselves, lovers of money, boastful, proud, abusive, unholy, lovers of pleasure, perverters of the Gospel of Christ, godless men, and Christ deniers (2 Thessalonians 2:3-4; 2 Timothy 3:1-4).

Sounds like the nation and times we live in, doesn't it?

Today, an ungodly evil force has besieged our land. We are no longer just fighting an invading army: Our foe has become an occupational force. It is entrenched in our homes and, sadly, most Christians have not stood watch. We haven't sounded the alarm or blown the trumpet.

If enemy soldiers ever invaded America, if they were in your city, on your street corner, would you and I simply sit back and watch or merely complain? No! We would do everything we could to defend ourselves, our loved ones, and our families, and to defeat the enemy. Well, it's time for action and, thank God, the battle is not over.

> Today, an ungodly evil force has besieged our land. We are no longer just fighting an invading army: Our foe has become an occupational force.

In a democracy, the majority is supposed to rule. I ask you, what do the majority of people in this nation really think about prayer in school? Or about being able to exhibit Judeo-Christian symbols such as the Ten Commandments or a Christmas manger scene in public places? Does the majority believe in the sanctity of life and that marriage is between one man and one woman? I believe they do! I believe *you* do, and it's time for the masses to shake off their apathy, be responsible, and get involved . . . based on the Word of God.

Many wonder, "Is it really possible for me to make a difference?" We can't sit back and do nothing. I'll say it again: *It's time to get involved.* We can't allow the liberal agenda, which I believe is motivated by spirits of darkness, to overtake us. We cannot just complain about how bad things have become. We need to take the responsibility and the offensive to bring about a change for righteousness. The transformation begins with a commitment from each one of us to be salt and light. We must permeate our culture at every point with the influence of the Gospel of the Kingdom of Jesus Christ.

What else can you do? You can follow the instructions of 2 Chronicles 7:14. You can repent and ask the Lord to forgive you. You can fast and pray for America. You can seek God's Throne for revival. You can pray for Him to give you discernment and Godly wisdom to know who to vote for. You can make sure you know the candidates' positions on the issues and cast your vote for those who will take a stand for righteousness in the decisions they make in office. And you can exercise one of the cherished freedoms you and I have: VOTE!

For many, your fathers and mothers, grandfathers and grandmothers, and even your sons and daughters fought to protect and preserve the freedoms we have in America. Precious lives have been sacrificed, their blood spilled on foreign soil, for this privilege. We used to say, "We hold these freedoms dear." Do we still? Does it anger you that so many Americans, especially Christians, neglect to register, and fail to vote, choosing to take their freedom for granted?

Let me remind you again of this disturbing statistic: In the last Presidential election less than 40% of Christians actually took the time to vote.

We must remember that the emblem of our faith is not a donkey, and it's not an elephant! In every election we need to unite behind the banner of the Cross and, together, vote for candidates – from the President of the United States to the city council member – who embrace the sanctity of life, who will protect marriage and family values, and who will honor prayer, the Ten Commandments, and God's Holy Word.

WILL YOU JOIN US?

Friend, it is extremely important who leads this nation. It matters greatly who our President, our governors, our senators, and our congressmen are. It's critical who is appointed to our courts.

It's time for the voices of the silent majority to be heard in the halls of our nation's government by your vote, and through your phone calls, emails, and letters to your elected officials.

Your voice must be heard in the Throne Room of God as you cry out to Him in humble repentance for His mercy rather than His judgment on America, for righteousness to abound and not godlessness and sin.

Some have said, "If God doesn't judge America, He is going to have to repent for destroying Sodom and Gomorrah," and you may ask, "Has America fallen that far?" I believe it has. When we allow a million unborn babies a year to be murdered...when we encourage homosexuality and attempt to pervert marriage instead of recognizing it as a holy union between one man and one woman...when crime, violence, hatred, drugs, materialism, and immorality run rampant and almost unchecked in our society...yes, we've fallen a long way from what God wants for us.

In truth, we *do* need to fall...to fall on our knees, that is. We must come before the Lord in repentance and pray for revival.

Remember, God told Abraham He would save the cities of Sodom and Gomorrah if He could find even 10 righteous people living there (Genesis 18). Won't He then spare the United States of America if we who are called by His name will humble ourselves before Him, repent of our sins and the sins of this nation, and choose to live lives characterized by Godly righteousness?

I'm asking you to join with Barbara and me and all of us here at Inspiration Ministries, as well as thousands of other friends, in fasting and in prayer for our nation! Together, let's pray for righteousness to be exalted, for a Godly President to sit in the Oval Office, and for virtuous leaders who will guide us in the paths of repentance and right living.

You hold the destiny of this nation in your hands... through your humility, your personal righteousness, your prayers, and your vote. Don't let others decide this nation's future. Take a stand for what is true, moral, and right in your prayer closet and at the ballot box.

At this critical time in our nation's history, we must repeat again and again the words of 2 Chronicles 7:14:

If my people who are called by My name humble themselves and pray and seek my face and turn from their wicked ways, then I will hear from heaven, will forgive their sin and will heal their land.

May God bless you – and may God bless this great nation, the United States of America – with a return to righteousness!

END NOTES

[1] Stuart Elliott, "Hey, Gay Spender, Marketers Spending Time With You," *New York Times,* June 26, 2006.

[2] Jane Spencer, "Coming Out: The Rise of Gay Cable Channels," *Wall Street Journal,* June 9, 2005.

[3] Barna Group, "A New Generation of Adults Bends Moral and Sexual Rules to Their Liking," www.barna.org, October 31, 2006.

[4] Gallup News Service, "Majority considers sex before marriage morally okay," April 5, 2001.

[5] Casey Williams, "MTV Smut Peddlers," Parents Television Council, 2005.

[6] "The Blue Tube: Foul Language on Prime Time Network TV," Parents Television Council, September 15, 2003.

[7] Bill Carter, "WB Censors Its Own Drama for Fear of F.C.C. Fines," *New York Times,* March 3, 2006.

[8] "Faith in a Box – Entertainment, Television & Religion 2005-2006," Parents Television Council, 2006.

[9] Media Life Magazine, "Survey: Two-Thirds Say Too Much Smut on TV," medialifemagazine.com, April 21, 2004.

[10] Parents Television Council, "Dying to Entertain – Violence on Prime Time Broadcast Television, 1998-2006," 2007.

[11] Media Week Magazine, "Arbitron: Consumers Want Uncensored Content," mediaweek.com, May 1, 2006.

[12] Reuters, "Sexy Media a Siren Call to Promiscuity?" www.reuters.com, April 3, 2006.

[13] Reuters, "TV to U.S. Govt: Hands Off Violent Programs," www.reuters.com, April 26, 2007.

[14] Associated Press, "Hollywood Doesn't Show Consequences," October 3, 2005.

[15] James Poniewozek, "Who Can Say What?" *Time Magazine,* April 12, 2007.

[16] Associated Press, "CBS Fires Don Imus From Radio Show," April 12, 2007.

[17] "A Deserved Bad Rap: Music's Impact," www.senate.gov/~brownback

[18] Associated Press, "Sexual Lyrics Prompt Teens to Have Sex," August 6, 2006.

[19] David Wooding, "'Homosexual' Is Banned," *The Sun,* April 20, 2007.

[20] Doug Huntington, "'Hate Crimes' Bill Hearings Begins Amid Christian Disapproval," *Christian Post,* April 19, 2007.

[21] Catherine Drinker Bowen, *Miracle At Philadelphia: The Story of the Constitutional Convention May - September 1787* (Boston: Back Bay Books, 1986).

[22] "Kin Beyond the Sea," William Gladstone, Leonard Roy Frank, eds, *Quotationary* (New York: Random House Reference, 2001).

[23] Dee Wampler, *The Myth of Separation Between Church and State* (Enumclaw: Winepress Publishing, 2004).

[24] James Reston, Jr., *Dogs of God* (New York: Doubleday, 2005).

[25] James A. Horn, *Land as God Made It* (New York: Basic Books, 2005).

[26] Paul A. Johnson, *History of the American People* (New York: Harper Perennial, 1997).

[27] "Spiritual Advice to Pilgrim Planters," Encyclopedia Britannica, The Annals of America, 1968 (Vol. 1).

[28] Paul Johnson, *A History of the American People* (New York: Harper Perennial, 1997).

29 Erik Bruun and Jay Crosby, eds, *Our Nation's Archive*, "Of Plymouth Plantation" by William Bradford, (New York: Tess Press, 1999).

30 William Bradford, "Of Plymouth Plantation," www.swarthmore.edu/SocSci/bdorsey1/41docs/14-bra.html

31 Paul Johnson, *A History of the American People* (New York: Harper Perennial, 1997).

32 Ibid.

33 William Hogeland, *The Whiskey Rebellion* (New York: Scribner, 2006).

34 Baker Publishing Group, *America's Great Revivals* (Minneapolis: Bethany House, 1994).

35 Robert Middlekauff, *The Glorious Cause* (New York: Oxford University Press, 2005).

36 Paul Johnson, *A History of the American People* (New York: Harper Perennial, 1997).

37 Dee Wampler, *The Myth of Separation Between Church and State* (Enumclaw: Winepress Publishing, 2004).

38 Ibid.

39 Catherine Marshall, *Beyond Ourselves*, (New York: Avon Books, 1961).

40 Michael and Jana Novak, *Washington's God* (New York: Basic Books, 2006).

41 Lewis Copeland, ed, *The World's Great Speeches* (New York: Garden City Publishing, 1942).

42 James H. Hutson, ed, *The Founding Fathers on Religion* (Princeton: Princeton University Press, 2005).

43 Ibid.

44 Adrienne Koch and William Peden, eds, "Notes on Virginia," *The Selected Writings of Thomas Jefferson* (New York: The Modern Library, 1944).

45 Gary DeMar, *On the Road to Independence* (Powder Springs: American Vision, 2005).

46 http://www.ushistory.org/declaration/related/dickinson.htm

47 James H. Hutson, ed, *The Founding Fathers on Religion* (Princeton: Princeton University Press, 2005).

48 Jonathan Z. Smith, ed, *The HarperCollins Dictionary of Religion* (San Francisco: HarperCollins, 1995).

49 Wesley L. Duewel, *Heroes of the Holy Life* (Grand Rapids: Zondervan, 2002).

50 W.P. Strickland, ed. *Autobiography of Peter Cartwright* (New York: Carlton & Porter, 1856), cited in "Peter Cartwright on Cane Ridge and the New Lights," http://www.piney.com/RMCart.html

51 Baker Publishing Group, *America's Great Revivals* (Minneapolis: Bethany House, 1994).

52 Ibid.

53 Charles Finney, *Revivals of Religion* (Virginia beach: CBN University Press, 1978); Louis P. Masur, "Revivals of Religion," *Year of Eclipse* (New York: Hill & Wang, 2001).

54 Alexis de Tocqueville, *Democracy in America* (Chicago: The Great Books Foundation, 1956).

55 Everett Dick, *The Sod-House Frontier 1854-1890* (Lincoln: University of Nebraska Press, 1979).

56 Peter Marshall and David Manuel, *Sounding Forth the Trumpet* (Grand Rapids: Fleming H. Revell, 2002).

57 R.A. Torrey, *Why God Used D. L. Moody* (New York: Fleming H. Revell, 1923).

CHOICES AND REWARDS
How to Live the Life God Loves to Bless

DO YOU EVER WONDER...

- Can God redeem your poor choices of the past?
- Do my daily choices matter to God?
- Am I doing enough for God's Kingdom?
- Are there Heavenly rewards based on my earthly choices?

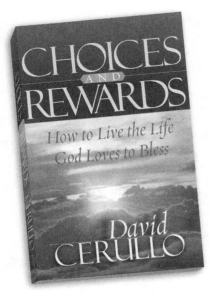

Choices and Rewards answers all of these questions and more. Receive teaching, encouragement, and inspiration to help you experience a new level of joy as you serve the Lord each day!

"Choices and Rewards was very inspiring and has made a great impact on me making the right choices in my life! Thank you." — SHIRLEY

For your gift of of $20 (£14) or more, we'll
God's Answers for Your Times of Trouble
in impacting the destiny of people

Write to David Cerullo, Inspiration Ministries
www.inspirationtoday.com to Sow your Seed for Souls and t

MINISTRY
RESOURCES

88 Jean-Paul Sartre, *Being and Nothingness* (New York: Washington Square Press, 1969); Ronald Hayman, Sarte: *A Biography* (New York: Carroll & Graf Publishers, 1987).

89 For more on the choices we make and their consequences, please read my book, *Choices and Rewards: How to Live the Life God Loves to Bless* (Charlotte: Inspiration Ministries, 2004).

90 Dee Wampler, *The Myth of Separation Between Church and State* (Enumclaw: Winepress Publishing, 2004).

91 Jon Meacham, *American Gospel* (New York: Random House, 2006).

92 Dee Wampler, *The Myth of Separation Between Church and State* (Enumclaw: Winepress Publishing, 2004).

93 David J. Brewer, *The United States: A Christian Nation* (Powder Springs: American Vision Publishing, 1996).

94 Ibid.

95 Adrienne Koch and William Peden, eds, *The Life and Selected Writings of Thomas Jefferson* (New York: The Modern Library, 1993).

96 Alan Sears and Craig Osten, *The ACLU vs. America* (Nashville: Broadman & Holman, 2005).

97 Robert Jeffress, *Hell? Yes!* (Colorado Springs: WaterBrook Press, 2004).

98 Barna Group, "How 'Christianized' Do Americans Want Their Country To Be?" www.barna.org (July 26, 2004); Albert L. Winseman, "Americans: Thou Shalt Not Remove the Ten Commandments," Gallup News Service, www.gallup.com (April 12, 2005); Frank Newport, "Americans Approve of Public Displays of Religious Symbols," Gallup News Service, www.gallup.com (October 3, 2006).

99 Alan Sears and Craig Osten, *The ACLU vs. America* (Nashville: Broadman & Holman, 2005).

100 Ibid.

101 Ibid.

102 Ibid.

103 Ibid.

104 James H. Hutson, ed, *The Founding Fathers on Religion* (Princeton: Princeton University Press, 2005).

105 Media Life Magazine, "Two-Thirds Say Too Much Smut on TV," www.medialifemagazine.com, April 22, 2004.

106 For more on the subject of spiritual warfare, please read my book, *Battle for Your Life!* (Charolotte: Inspiration Ministries, 2006).

107 PRWEB, "World Muslim Leader Rejects Pope's Comment on Jihad," www.prweb.com, September 17, 2006.

108 "Discovery of the New World – Christopher Columbus." *Encyclopedia Britannica,* The Annals of America. 1968. (Vol. 1).

[58] Gordon Leidner, "Religious Revival in Civil War Armies," Great American History, http://www.greatamericanhistory.net/revival.htm

[59] Shelby Foote, *The Civil War: Fort Sumter to Perryville* (New York: Vintage Books, 1986).

[60] James Hawkinson, ed, *Glad Hearts* (Chicago: Covenant Publications, 2003) of "G.D. Hall, Pastor-Journalist: Reports Mission Meetings 1895-1911," George F. Hall (typed manuscript, 1991).

[61] Elmer L. Towns and Douglas Porter Servant Publications, "The Ten Greatest Revivals Ever," www.elmertowns.com/books/preview/10_great_revivals/10_Greatest_Revivals_Ever.

[62] Wesley Duewel, *Heroes of the Holy Life* (Grand Rapids: Zondervan, 2002).

[63] Frank Bartleman, *Azusa Street* (Plainfield: Logos International, 1980).

[64] Barna Group, "Practical Outcomes Replace Biblical Principles as the Moral Standard," www.barna.org (September 10, 2001).

[65] George H. Gallup Jr., "War Changed Prayer Habits of Many Americans," Gallup News Service, www.gallup.com (July 29, 2003).

[66] Gary DeMar, *Building a City on a Hill* (Powder Springs: American Vision, 2005).

[67] David McCullough, *John Adams* (New York: Simon & Schuster, 2001).

[68] William J. Federer, *American Minute* (St. Louis: AmeriSearch, 2004).

[69] William Federer, ed, *America's God and Country* (St. Louis: AmeriSearch, 1996).

[70] Conrad Black, *Franklin Delano Roosevelt* (New York: Public Affairs, 2003).

[71] David McCullough, *Truman* (New York: Simon & Schuster, 1992).

[72] Will Durant, *The Life of Greece* (New York: Simon & Schuster, 1939).

[73] Frank Newport, "Twenty-Eight Percent Believe Bible Is Actual Word of God," Gallup News Service, www.gallup.com (May 22, 2006).

[74] Cathy Lynn Grossman, "Americans Get an 'F' in Religion," *USA Today*, April 8, 2007.

[75] Barna Group, "A New Generation of Adults Bends Moral and Sexual Rules to Their Liking," www.barna.org (October 31, 2006).

[76] Barna Group, "Born Again Christians Ignorant of Faith; Survey Also Finds Hell's Description Divides Americans," www.barna.org (March 31, 1996).

[77] Harris Interactive Poll, "Many Americans Not 'Absolutely Certain' Of God," November 11, 2006.

[78] Frank Newport, "A Look at Religious Switching in America Today," Gallup News Service, www.gallup.com (June 23, 2006).

[79] Lydia Saad, "Morality Ratings the Worst in Five Years," Gallup News Service, www.gallup.com (May 25, 2006).

[80] Rosemary Goring, ed, *Larousse's Dictionary of Beliefs & Religions* (New York: Larousse, 1994).

[81] Robert Jeffress, *Hell? Yes!* (Colorado Springs: WaterBrook Press, 2004).

[82] Ibid.

[83] Ibid.

[84] Ibid.

[85] Barna Group, "Virginia Tech Tragedy Is a Wake-Up Call to Parents," www.barna.org (April 23, 2007).

[86] Walter Kaufmann, trans, *Thus Spake Zarathustra,* Friedrich Nietzsche (New York: Viking Press, 1968).

[87] Bertrand Russell, *The Basic Writings of Bertrand Russell 1903-1959,* "What Is an Agnostic?" (New York: Clarion Books, 1967).

"BATTLE FOR YOUR LIFE"
VICTORY PACK *Will Give Your*
the Tools You Need to Triumph
Over the Enemy!

This powerful array of spiritual resources includes:

- *Battle for Your Life.* This timely manual will equip you to pull down enemy strongholds so you can discover God's destiny for your life!

- **Three video DVDs** of a teaching series on spiritual warfare. You'll want to watch the DVDs with your family, small group, or Sunday school class.

- **The audio CDs** of messages are a wonderful resource to listen to in your car, helping you put on the *"full armor of God"* each day!

- A **bookmark** to remind you of key Biblical principles for gaining victory over Satan. Keep it in your Bible or in your copy of the *Battle for Your Life* book!

Do You Need a MIRACLE from God?

Does it feel as though all hell has broken loose in your life? Are you convinced it would take a miracle for your circumstances to change? If so, I have good news for you today:

God is a God of MIRACLES!

Our loving Heavenly Father is the same yesterday, today, and forever, and He has never stopped intervening in His children's lives with His mighty, life-changing miracles!

Do you need God's supernatural intervention today in your...

BODY, SOUL, OR SPIRIT?
FINANCES, HOME, OR JOB?
MARRIAGE, CHILDREN,
OR FRIENDSHIPS?

How to Receive Your Miracle from God is a book that will help you experience the miracle you need from Him!

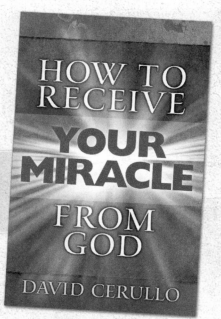

Get ready to receive YOUR miracle!

"How to Receive Your Miracle tells me how to look forward to God's promises for complete healing in my life. This book has been an eye opener for me to the keys of living!" — KAREN

For a gift of $20 (£10) this powerful tool will be sent to you in appreciation for your partnership in our ministry.

Visit www.inspirationtoday.com, or ca

HOPE FOR *Your* NEW BEGINNING

I n the midst of the winter seasons and storms of life, God wants to fill you with His peace, hope, and joy! If you're facing a difficult situation— an illness, the loss of a loved one, a financial setback, or struggles with your children—God wants to give you a New Beginning!

If you need a New Beginning in your...

Marriage • Job • Health
Finances • Children

God wants to step into the circumstances of your life with His supernatural breakthroughs.

Hope For Your New Beginning book and audio CD will provide the tools you need to experience victory and abundance in Christ.

"I was blessed by your book New Beginnings. This is such a profound word from the heart of God, and I have asked the Lord to order my steps into His New Beginning. I want all the miracles and new beginnings He has ordained for my life and for my family's life this year and for years to come." — INGRID

God Answers Prayer!

"If two of you agree on earth concerning anything that they ask, it will be done for them by My Father in Heaven." – MATTHEW 18:19

"Thanks so much for your prayers for my husband Michael, who had been diagnosed with cancer. Michael went back for a check-up, and the doctor said his cancer is GONE! Praise the Lord!" – HELEN

"Your prayers and those of our friends have brought Divine healing to my mom's thyroid disease! She's returned to her former health!" – JAMES

"My wife's back was healed when your prayer minister agreed with me in prayer!" – ALLEN

"Thank you for your prayers! I've received a total healing regarding high blood pressure and a possible stroke." – IBIRONKE

Our prayer ministers welcome the opportunity to agree together with you in prayer and believe God to step into the circumstances of your life with His supernatural power!

Visit our website at www.inspirationtoday.com and click on "Prayer Request," or call 704-943-3300 Monday through Friday from 8:00 a.m. to 5 p.m. (EST).

"Thank you for having one of your Prayer Ministers call and pray with me today. The call came at just the right time, and it made me feel like someone really cares. Again, thank you for the call just to pray with me." — GLORIA